CIRCULATORY SYSTEM

RUTH BJORKLUND

mc Marshall Cavendish
Benchmark

Marshall Cavendish Benchmark
99 White Plains Roads
Tarrytown, New York 10591
www.marshallcavendish.us

Editor: Karen Ang
Publisher: Michelle Bisson
Art Director: Anahid Hamparian
Series Designer: Kay Petronio
Library of Congress Cataloging-in-Publication Data
Bjorklund, Ruth.
Circulatory system / by Ruth Bjorklund.
p. cm. — (The amazing human body)
Includes bibliographical references and index.
Summary: "Discusses the parts that make up the human circulatory system,
what can go wrong, how to treat those illnesses and diseases, and how to
stay healthy"—Provided by publisher.
ISBN 978-0-7614-3053-7
1. Cardiovascular system—Juvenile literature. I. Title.
QP103.B56 2009
612.1—dc22
2007050436

 = red blood cells

Photo research by Tracey Engel
Front cover photo: Phototake Inc. / Alamy
The photographs in this book are used by permission and through the courtesy of:
Alamy: Phototake Inc., 1, 4, 6, 14, 15, 25, 33, 34, 38, 43, 51, 56, 58; Nucleus Medical Art, Inc., 9, 22, 26, 28, 44; Peter Arnold, Inc., 16; Dennis MacDonald, 17; WoodyStock, 49; Medical-on-Line, 50. *Photo Researchers, Inc.:* Steve Gschmeissner, 7; BSIP, 10; Susumu Nishinaga, 11; Martin M. Rotker, 13; John Bavosi, 20, 46; SPL, 29; Ian Hooton, 30; Dick Luria, 36; Mauro Fermariello, 41; Michelle Del Guercio, 54; Gérard Villaréal, 70; Gary Carlson, back cover. *Corbis:* Jens Nieth/zefa, 12; John Henley, 71. *Phototake:* BSIP, 45. *Shutterstock:* Dario Sabljak, 48; Hisom Silviu, 60; Dana Heinemann, 62; Tom Oliverira, 63; PhotoCreate, 68; Jose Gill, 69. *USDA:* 65. *Envision:* Mark Ferri, 66.

Printed in China
123456

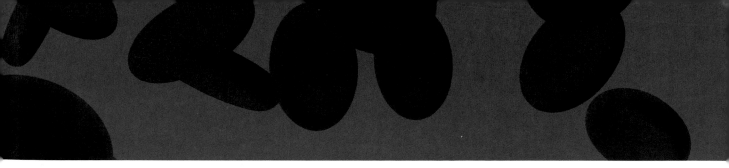

CONTENTS

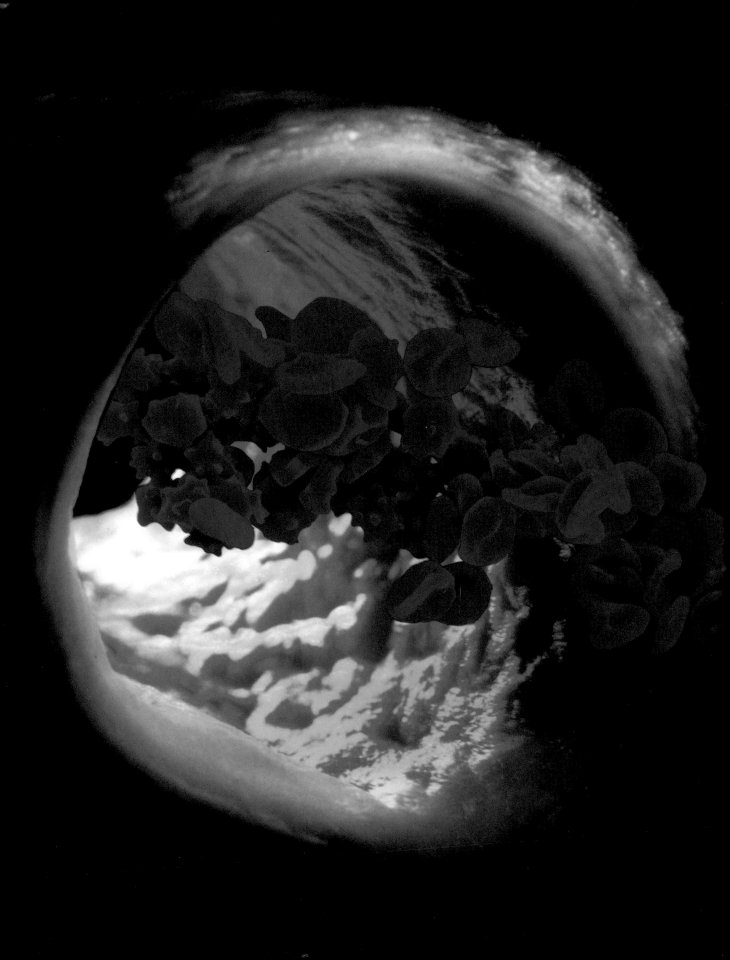

1

What Is the Human Circulatory System?

The human circulatory system works with other body systems to supply oxygen and nutrients to the entire body. Composed of three basic parts—heart, blood vessels, and blood—the circulatory system performs an unrelenting, life-giving task each living moment. The heart, the body's hardest-working muscle, pumps blood to the lungs and then to the body through a complex network of blood vessels. Traveling in a one-way circuit, or route, blood distributes nourishment to the cells and tissues and carries away waste.

The circulatory system gets its name from the way blood circulates throughout the body's network of blood vessels.

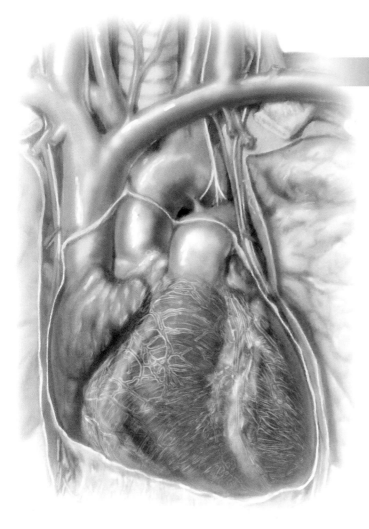

In children, the heart is about the size of a fist. But in adults, the heart is twice that size.

THE HEART

An essential organ of the human body, a healthy heart weighs less than a pound (.45 kilograms), and is approximately 5.5 inches (14 centimeters) tall by 3.5 inches (9 cm) wide by 2.5 inches (6 cm) thick. It is supported by ligaments attached to the sternum, or breastbone, and hangs slightly to the left of the center of the chest.

The walls of the heart are composed of three layers—epicardium, myocardium, and endocardium. The epicardium is the thin outer layer of tissue and fat. Surrounding the epicardium is a protective two-layer sac called the pericardium. This sac anchors the heart in position and holds fluid inside its layers. This fluid lubricates the heart and helps to keep it running smoothly. The inner layer of the wall of the heart is called the endocardium. This is a very smooth layer made up of endothelial cells, which are also found in the inner linings of blood vessels. The endocardium keeps the blood flowing smoothly and controls the heart as it forms before a baby is born. The endocardium also helps regulate heartbeats. The thickest and strongest wall of the heart is the middle layer, or myocardium. The myocardium is made of unique muscle called cardiac muscle.

Muscles

There are three types of muscle in the body: skeletal, smooth, and cardiac. Skeletal muscle is striated, which means the muscle fibers occur in layers. Skeletal muscles, such as those found in the legs or hands, are voluntary. In other words, these voluntary muscles contract and relax when told to do so by electrical stimuli from the brain. Movements such as walking or writing are carried out by voluntary skeletal muscles. The second type of muscle is smooth muscle. This muscle is found on the inside of major organs in the body. Its movement is involuntary, or automatic. Examples of this are muscle contractions that take place inside the intestines as the body digests food.

Cardiac muscle is different from the other muscle types in that it is striated like skeletal muscle, but automatic like smooth muscle. Unlike other muscles, heart muscle does not need to rest. It operates constantly.

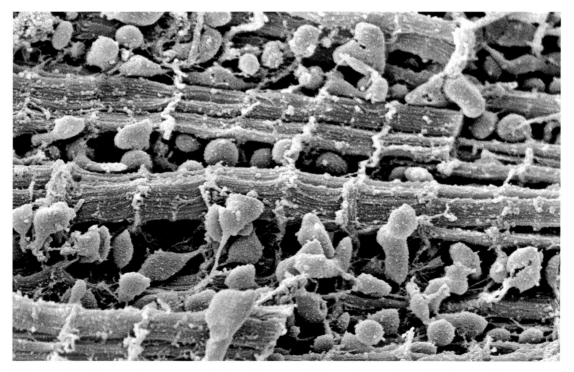

This magnified image shows a sample of cardiac muscle from a human heart. The layers of muscle fibers (blue) create the striations.

Cardiac muscles are connected to one another by strands of fibers called intercalated discs. The discs help strengthen cardiac muscles and prevent them from tearing. Inside the intercalated discs, molecules travel freely, allowing the cardiac muscle cells to communicate electrically with one another.

Chambers

The heart is a hollow organ with four flexible and resilient inner chambers. The upper two chambers are called the atria. Singly, one is called an atrium, from the Latin word meaning "entrance." The lower chambers are called the ventricles, from the Latin word for "belly." The heart is also divided into two sides—left and right. The two sides are separated by a wall of muscle tissue called the septum. The septum prevents blood on one side from mixing with blood on the other. It is critical that the two sides remain apart because the two sides of the heart perform completely separate functions.

Valves

Valves also play a crucial role in circulating blood. The four valves of the heart are flaps of tissue that open and close to keep the blood flowing in one direction and prevent blood from backing up. The valves located between the atria and the ventricles are called atrioventricular valves. The two valves that connect the ventricles to the arteries are called aortic semilunar valves. The atrioventricular valve between the right atrium and the right ventricle is called the tricuspid valve, while the one between the left atrium and left ventricle is called the mitral valve. The sound of the valves opening and closing is what one hears when listening for a heartbeat.

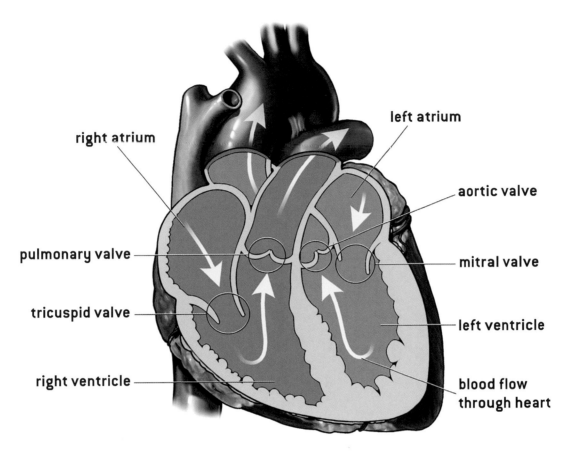

right atrium

left atrium

aortic valve

pulmonary valve

mitral valve

tricuspid valve

left ventricle

right ventricle

blood flow
through heart

The atrioventricular valves get their names from their shape. The flap that forms the tricuspid valve is made of three curves that meet at one point or cusp. The mitral valve is named after the miter or headwear used by bishops and other religious leaders. The mitral valve's shape resembles this headwear.

BLOOD VESSELS

Blood vessels are the system of hollow tubes that carry blood to and from the heart. If they could be set end to end, they would extend for more than 60,000 miles. There are three types of blood vessels: arteries, veins, and capillaries. Arteries carry blood *away* from the heart and veins carry blood *to* the heart. Capillaries connect the two systems. Blood vessels are composed of layers of flexible tissue.

Arteries

Arteries are the strongest, thickest, and most elastic of all the vessels. Arteries have three layers. The inner lining is called the intima and it contains a thin, smooth layer of endothelial cells. The middle layer, called the media, is made of strong muscle fibers that wrap around the vessels and can readily stretch to accommodate the pressure of pumping blood. When the heart beats, the media layer expands, stays stretched out, and then relaxes. This movement can be felt by touching the thin skin of the wrists, temples, and behind the knees. It is called the pulse. The outer layer of the arteries, the externa, is made of connective tissue that surrounds and protects the movements of the media layer.

A test called an angiogram can show doctors the blood vessels in different parts of a person's body.

The largest artery is called the aorta. It rises upward after leaving the left ventricle of the heart, and forms an arch that extends downward to the abdomen and separates into two arteries. All major arteries leaving the heart, except the pulmonary artery, branch off from the aorta. The first to do so are the left and right coronary arteries. These vessels are connected to the upward, or ascending, aorta. Coronary arteries carry oxygen-rich blood to the heart itself. Other arteries that stem from the aortic arch are the brachiocephalic artery, the left common carotid artery, and the left subclavian artery.

Arteries that branch from the descending aorta are the thoracic and abdominal arteries, which split into large arteries that branch into medium sized arteries. Arteries branch off into smaller arteries, called arterioles. Arterioles control the flow of blood into the smallest vessels, the capillaries.

Capillaries

Capillaries are tiny, thin-walled vessels that form a network throughout the body. It is here, in this web of blood vessels, sometimes called the capillary bed, that the blood's nutrients and oxygen supply are exchanged for carbon dioxide and cell waste. Capillaries are formed by a single layer of smooth endothelial cells, surrounded by a protective coating. The pathways are so narrow that blood travels through a single red blood cell at a time.

Veins

The venous system, or network of veins, collects cell waste and carries it back to the heart. Blood circulates in only one direction around the body. As it does so, the wastes and carbon dioxide exchanged in the capillaries join the circulatory flow in the smallest veins, called venules. The venous system consists of the venules, medium-sized veins, larger veins, and the superior and inferior venae cavae, the two largest veins.

Vein walls are flexible, but they are not as strong as arteries because they do not need to withstand the force

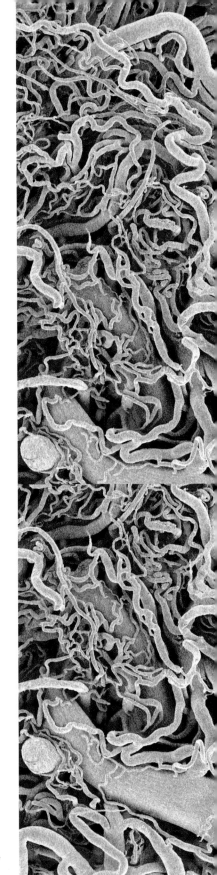

Blood vessels of varying widths and lengths form a complex network throughout the body.

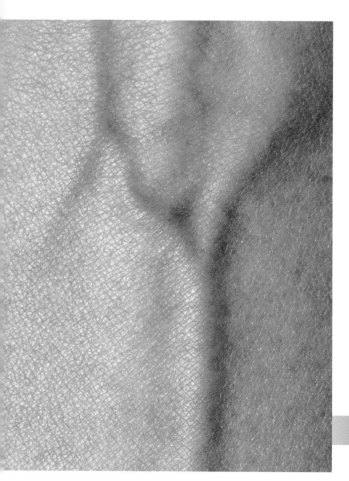

Some veins and arteries can be seen through the skin. The back of your hand is one place to look for them.

of arterial blood pressure. By the time blood reaches the veins, blood pressure is greatly reduced. In order to finish the venous circuit, veins depend on contractions made by skeletal muscles in the arms, legs, and lungs to assist in blood flow. Larger veins have a series of valves that open and close to maintain the one-way flow of blood and to keep the blood from pooling. As blood moves through the veins, it eventually empties into one of the two venae cavae, the superior vena cava or the inferior vena cava. Both empty into the right atrium.

BLOOD

Connective tissue is one of four types of tissue found in the body, and is defined as tissue that gives structure and support to organs. Blood is the only human connective tissue that is fluid. Whole blood is made up of red blood cells, white blood cells, and platelets. These cells are suspended in liquid called plasma. Each portion of whole blood contributes to the nourishment of the body. An adult human body has about 5 quarts (4.7 liters) of whole blood flowing through its system of arteries and veins.

In order to examine the composition of whole blood, a sample of blood is collected in a vial and placed in a machine called a centrifuge. The centrifuge spins at high speeds, causing the blood to separate into its different parts. Whole blood in the centrifuged vial separates into three layers. The largest layer is the plasma, a clear yellowish fluid. Red blood cells make up about 40 to 45 percent of the blood sample. The remaining layer, which is only a small portion of the total, is called the "buffy coat" because of its buff, or orange-yellow, color. This is a mixture of platelets and most of the white blood cells.

There are more than 25 trillion erythrocytes, or red blood cells, contained in the blood of the human body. The major role of red blood cells is to deliver oxygen and remove carbon dioxide. Red blood cells, or RBCs as they are sometimes called, have an unusual form and structure. Since they are flat and slightly curved, they can easily bend and fold through capillary openings. At the center of each red blood cell is hemoglobin, a protein that stores oxygen and other gases. As the blood flows, the hemoglobin in the red blood cells releases oxygen to cells and tissues through-

The test tube on the left has whole blood. The tube on the right shows blood that has been separated into its three main layers.

out the body. In an exchange of gases, the oxygen is given to the cells, and the cells give back carbon dioxide as waste. Carbon dioxide is carried to the lungs, where it is exhaled out of the body. Because it is composed of iron-rich molecules, hemoglobin gives blood its red color.

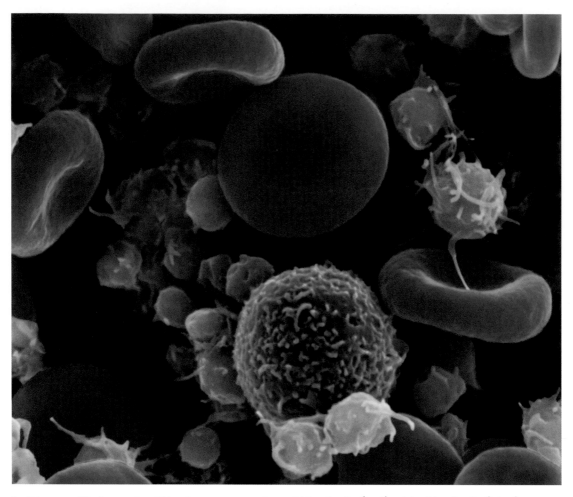

In this magnified sample of blood you can see the red blood cells (red), white blood cells (blue), and platelets (yellow).

There are several types of white blood cells, or leukocytes, that circulate in whole blood. White blood cells have an unusual shape that allows them to squeeze in and out of blood vessels and cellular walls. Though larger than red blood cells, white blood cells make up a tiny portion of the volume of whole blood. However, white blood cells perform the important task of defending the body against foreign substances, disease, and infection.

Platelets are suspended in the plasma along with white blood cells. These cells help blood clot, or stick together. Together, white blood cells and platelets make up less than one percent of whole blood.

About 55 percent of whole blood is a sticky, yellow-colored fluid called plasma. Plasma is about 90 percent water. What remains in plasma besides water are essential nutrients, vitamins, minerals, medicines, hormones, proteins, and waste products.

Blood Type

Even though all human blood is composed of plasma, red blood cells, white blood cells, and platelets, all human blood is not exactly the same. There are four distinct blood types: A, B, AB, and O. Blood types refer to a combination of antigens and antibodies that may or may not be present in the blood. Antigens are attached to

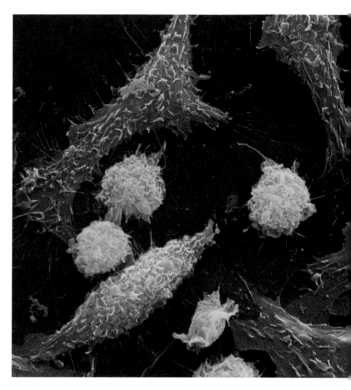

There are many different types of white blood cells. Macrophages (brown) surround and destroy invading substances or dead cells. Lymphocytes (yellow-green) trigger immune responses.

red blood cells and aid in the production of antibodies. There are two antigens, and they are labeled A or B. The antibodies they produce are found in plasma. Antibodies attack and destroy foreign substances that do not belong in the body, such as bacteria or viruses. However, a specific antibody will also attack antigens that did not aid in the production of that antibody.

Blood type is determined by the presence or lack of the A or B antigen. For example, if a person has A antigens attached to his or her red blood cells, then there will be antibodies to fight off the B antigen in the plasma. That person is said to have Type A blood. If a person has B antigens on the red blood cells, then there will be antibodies to fight the A antigen in the plasma That person will have Type B blood. A person with both the

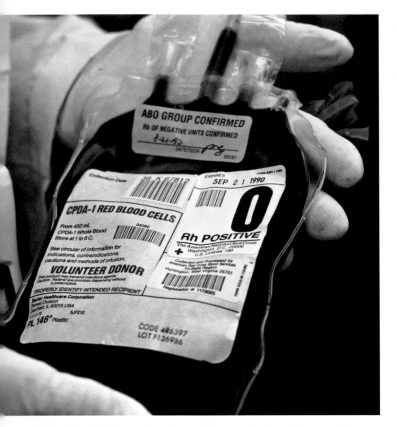

Blood that is donated and used for transfusions is stored in sterile—or clean—bags and refrigerated.

A and the B antigens is said to have Type AB blood. People with AB blood have no antibodies in the plasma, but they have A and B antigens. The person with Type O blood (which is called Type 0 [zero] in many other countries) has no antigens on the red blood cells. But both A and B antibodies are present in the plasma.

There is a third antigen that affects blood type called the Rhesus D antigen or Rh(D) factor. Most people have the Rhesus D antigen present, and they are said to be Rh(D) positive, or RH+. If the antigen is absent, then a person is said to be Rh(D) negative, or RH-. Human blood types are expressed in terms of the ABO blood type and the positive or negative condition of the Rh(D) factor. So people with A antigens and Rhesus D antigens on their red blood cells are said to have Type A positive blood. A different example would be people with no antigens on their red blood cells. Their blood type would be Type O negative. Type A positive and Type O positive are the most common blood types. Less than 3 percent of the population has Type AB blood.

When a person suffers blood loss, the blood supply must be replenished. If the loss is severe, the quickest and most effective way to restore the blood is a blood transfusion. Blood for transfusions comes from the generosity of people who donate their blood at blood banks, hospitals, or during blood drives at community centers. Once blood has been collected, the red

DONATING BLOOD

Having a ready supply of blood is critical to everyone's health. Blood may be needed when a person has an accident or injury, has surgery, or is affected by a large-scale disaster, such as a hurricane or an earthquake. The only way to have blood on hand for such emergencies is to collect blood from donors.

Blood is most often collected at blood banks or blood drives. A blood blank is a community medical center that collects, tests, and stores blood that is later distributed to different hospitals. A blood drive is an event where—at a prearranged time and place—a bloodmobile visits a community location, such as a school, grocery store, church, or other public area. A bloodmobile is a medical clinic built inside a large van or bus.

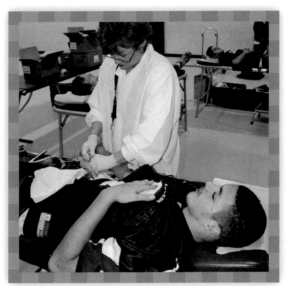

Donating blood is quite easy and very safe. It only takes a few minutes to register and answer some health questions, and then another ten to fifteen minutes for the nurse to to draw the blood. After donating blood, donors are given a little refreshment and offered a comfortable area to recover. To donate blood, a person must be at least 17 years old, weigh at least 110 pounds (about 50 kg), and be in good general health. An adult has between 10 to 12 pints (4.7 to 5.6 liters) of blood and a blood donor gives 1 pint (around 0.5 l) of whole blood at a time. It usually takes four to eight weeks to regenerate the lost blood. During that time, donors should follow an iron-rich diet or take iron tablets.

After blood is donated, it is processed at a lab. First, the blood is carefully screened for any diseases or abnormalities. If the blood is healthy, then it is further processed and divided by blood type and Rh factor. Some whole blood is stored, but much of the blood is separated into units of red blood cells, plasma, and platelets. Whole blood can be stored for forty-two days, plasma can be frozen and stored for a year, but platelets, must be thrown out after just five days. In the United States, more than 35,000 units of blood are used every day. With such a short storage time for fresh blood, it is critical that blood donors volunteer as often and as much as they can.

Check online to locate a blood bank or to find out when a blood drive will be in your community.

blood cells are separated from the plasma. Medical facilities can store the red blood cells for up to forty-two days. When a blood transfusion is needed, blood that has been drawn from a donor is injected into a recipient. But donor blood must be compatible with the recipient's blood. A transfusion can save a life, but using the wrong type of blood can kill. Health care workers thoroughly inspect blood type when performing transfusions.

Antigens attached to the red blood cells from the donor remain in the stored blood. These antigens will react with any antibodies already present in the recipient's plasma. A recipient is able to receive blood that is exactly their type. In some cases they can also receive other kinds of blood. For example, a person with Type A blood will have antibodies against Type B blood, and the same is true in reverse. So both can donate to people with Type AB blood, since people with Type AB blood have no antibodies in their plasma. People with Type AB blood can receive blood from anyone, and their blood type is known as the "universal recipient." But Type AB blood carries both A and B antigens on its red blood cells, so it cannot be donated to anyone except those with Type AB blood. Conversely, Type O is called the "universal donor." Since Type O blood carries no antigens on the red blood cells, anyone can receive this blood. But because people with Type O carry both antibodies in their plasma, they can receive blood only from other Type O donors.

There is more to matching blood types than the ABO compatibility. The Rh(D) antigen must also be determined before a blood transfusion. Most people are Rh(D) positive, meaning that they carry the antigen and not the antibody against it. So people who are Rh(D) positive can receive positive or negative blood. However, if you have Rh(D) negative blood, you can receive only negative blood. Of all possible blood types, Type O negative blood, though rather rare, is the truest "universal donor" and the type most valued by blood banks.

BLOOD DONATION AT A GLANCE

If your blood type is		
TYPE	**YOU CAN GIVE BLOOD TO**	**YOU CAN RECEIVE BLOOD FROM**
A+	A+ AB+	A+ A– O+ O–
O+	O+ A+ B+ AB+	O+ O–
B+	B+ AB+	B+ B– O+ O–
AB+	AB+	Everyone
A–	A+ A– AB+ AB–	A- O-
O–	Everyone	O–
B–	B+ B– AB+ AB–	B– O–
AB–	AB+ AB–	AB– A– B– O–

Of each 100 Americans

84 donors are Rh(D)+	16 donors are Rh(D)–
38 are O+	7 are O–
34 are A+	6 are A–
9 are B+	2 are B–
3 are AB+	1 is AB–

Charts are based on information from the American Association of Blood Banks (http://www.aabb.org)

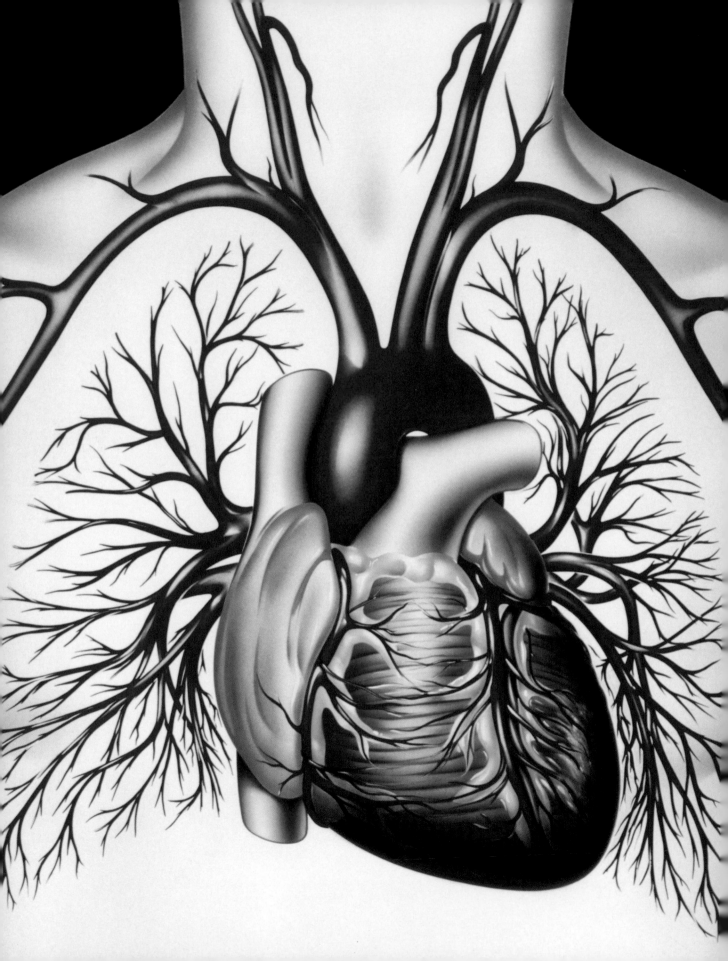

2

How the Circulatory System Works

Over the course of a single day, the heart beats more than one hundred thousand times, pushing the equivalent of 2,000 gallons (7.6 kiloliters) of blood through the body's network of blood vessels. This blood nourishes every single one of the more than 50 trillion cells in the human body.

◀ With duties that include constantly pumping blood, heart muscles are some of the hardest-working muscles in the entire body.

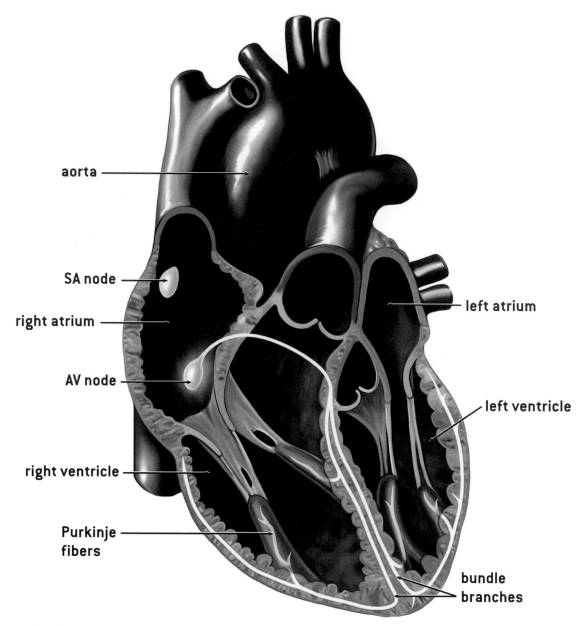

aorta

SA node

right atrium

AV node

right ventricle

Purkinje fibers

left atrium

left ventricle

bundle branches

The SA and AV nodes are responsible for stimulating the heart muscles.

THE CIRCUITS OF THE HEART

The heart is a unique, muscular pump. Its four chambers beat in a highly synchronized, two-stage motion. To function, the heart requires electrical stimulation, but unlike other muscles that receive electrical signals from the brain telling them to contract and relax, the heart muscle stimulates itself. Certain cells of the heart, commonly called pacemaker cells, are located in two areas, or nodes, called the sinoatrial node (SA node) and the atrioventricular node (AV node). To produce the heart's muscle contractions, the cells in the upper node, the SA node, initiate an electrical impulse and pass it on to nearby cells and to muscle fibers called Purkinje fibers. The Purkinje fibers form an electrical pathway for the impulse to travel to the lower AV node. The AV node spreads the electricity to the lower chambers of the heart, assisted by a bundle of fibers. These fibers are called the bundle of His, and are named after Wilhelm His Jr, the first scientist to describe them.

With each impulse, the muscles of the heart contract, and the movement pushes blood to all areas of the body. The pacemaker cells in the SA node set the pace for the heart by creating electrical impulses 60 to 100 times a minute. The impulse spreads, slowed down somewhat by the AV node, which pulses at 40 to 60 times a minute. The difference between the SA node's and the AV node's impulses makes the heart beat in a slight ripple motion. On average, the heart beats 70 times a minute, making the entire process of conducting electricity through the heart less than one second long.

The four chambers of the heart pump in unison, but perform very separate tasks. The heart pumps in two phases, the systole and the diastole. Systole is the beat and diastole is the rest. The atrial systole, or contraction, is milder and slightly precedes the ventricular systole, which is much more powerful. As blood enters the heart, the atria expand to accommodate the volume. Then the atria contract and pump the blood to the ventricles. Before the ventricular systole, the ventricles expand to receive the blood from the atria. The ventricles then contract, pushing the blood out of the heart. The semilunar valves—between the ventricles and the arteries leaving the heart—close to keep the blood from flowing backward into the ventricles. The heart takes a brief rest called diastole, which allows the blood to re-fill the chambers. The process begins again.

HEART SOUNDS

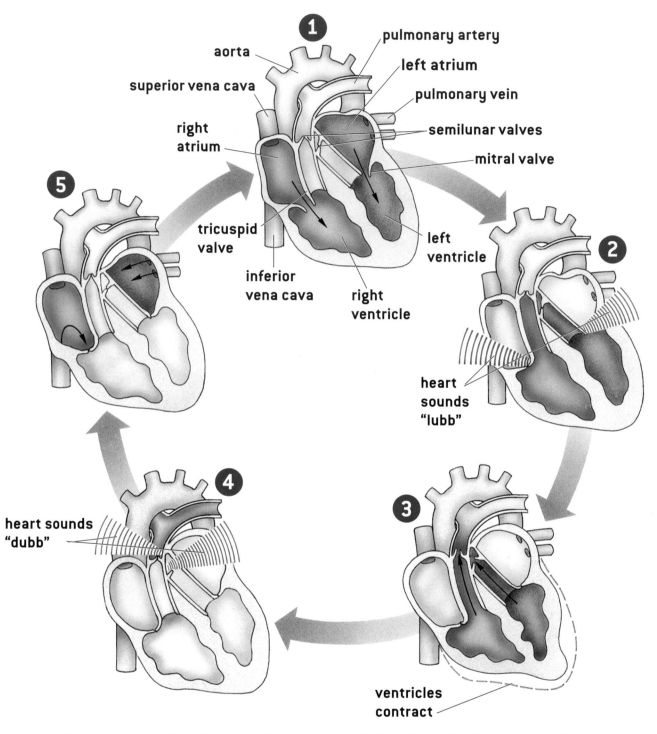

The sound of normal heartbeats are often described as "lubb-dubb." In a healthy heart, blood flows from the atria into the ventricles (1), causing the tricuspid and mitral valves to close. This produces the "lubb" sound (2). The ventricles contract (3) and push the blood out of the ventricles into the pulmonary artery and aorta. The semilunar valves close, causing the "dubb" sound (4). The atria refill with blood from the vena cavae and the pulmonary vein, and the process repeats (5).

The heart is responsible for pumping blood through three complete circuits, or routes. These are the pulmonary circuit, the cardiac circuit, and the systemic circuit.

The Pulmonary Circuit

In the pulmonary circuit, blood carrying cell waste arrives at the right atrium of the heart. It enters through two large veins, the superior vena cava, which carries oxygen-poor blood from the upper part of the body, and the inferior vena cava, which brings in oxygen-poor blood from the lower body and legs. The blood fills the right atrium, causing the atrium to swell. Then the atrium contracts to push the blood into the right ventricle. The tricuspid valve between the right atrium and the right ventricle, closes behind the flow, keeping the blood contained. Then the right ventricle expands with the incoming blood and pumps it into the main pulmonary artery. The pulmonary semilunar valve closes shut to prevent the blood from backwashing into the heart.

Blood flows into the pulmonary artery, which leaves the heart and branches into left and right pulmonary arteries that enter into the left and right lungs. In the lungs, oxygen-rich air is stored in a series of passageways

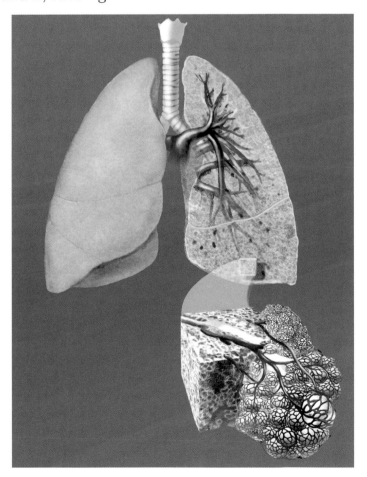

Alveoli have many small blood capillaries that are important for the oxygen exchange.

that separate and become progressively smaller. The smallest passage-ways are thin-walled air sacs called alveoli. The alveoli are wrapped in blood capillaries. When the alveoli fill with air, oxygen passes through the alveoli cell walls to the capillaries. The oxygen molecules bind with the hemoglobin in the red blood cells inside the capillaries. The red blood cells transfer carbon dioxide, the waste gas produced by the cells in the rest of the body, back through the cell walls and into the alveoli. (This carbon dioxide is breathed out of the lungs in exhalations.)

Reoxygenated blood travels out of the lungs through pulmonary veins. To complete the pulmonary circuit, four main pulmonary veins enter into the left atrium of the heart. It is important to remember that the pulmonary arteries carry oxygen-poor blood and the pulmonary

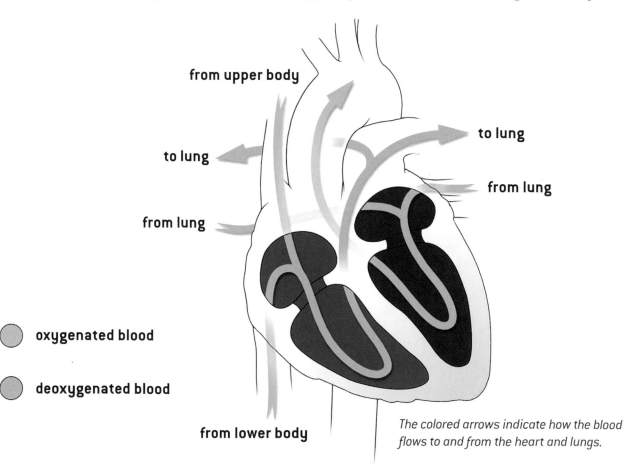

from upper body

to lung

to lung

from lung

from lung

oxygenated blood

deoxygenated blood

from lower body

The colored arrows indicate how the blood flows to and from the heart and lungs.

veins carry oxygen-rich blood. Elsewhere in the circulatory system, arteries carry oxygen-rich blood, and veins transport oxygen-poor blood.

The Cardiac Circuit

The cardiac circuit is the smallest in distance and serves to nourish the heart itself. The circuit begins with coronary arteries branching off of the ascending aorta. These vessels curve back to the walls of the heart, and separate into capillaries which feed into coronary veins that return deoxygenated blood back to the heart.

The Systemic Circuit

The systemic circuit is the extensive journey of the blood through the body and back to the heart. As newly oxygenated blood enters the left atrium through the pulmonary veins, the left atrium pushes the blood down into the left ventricle. The mitral valve, between the left atrium and the left ventricle, closes while the left ventricle fills. As the left ventricle contracts, it pushes blood into the aorta, and the aortic semilunar valve closes. The blood begins its circuit around the body. The blood must reach all parts of the body, so the force of the contraction of the left ventricle is much stronger than the right. As a result, the left side of the heart is larger and stronger.

The aorta, as the first recipient of this force, must withstand the pressure of the blood as it rushes out of the left ventricle. The aorta is thick—nearly an inch across—making it the largest artery in the body. Arteries that branch from the portion of the aorta called the ascending aorta, are the brachiocephalic artery, the left carotid artery, and the left subclavian artery. These deliver blood to the upper body. The right carotid artery branches off of the brachiocephalic artery and travels up the right side of the neck to bring oxygenated blood to the neck, eyes, and brain. The left carotid artery, which branches directly from the aorta, delivers

The Circulatory System

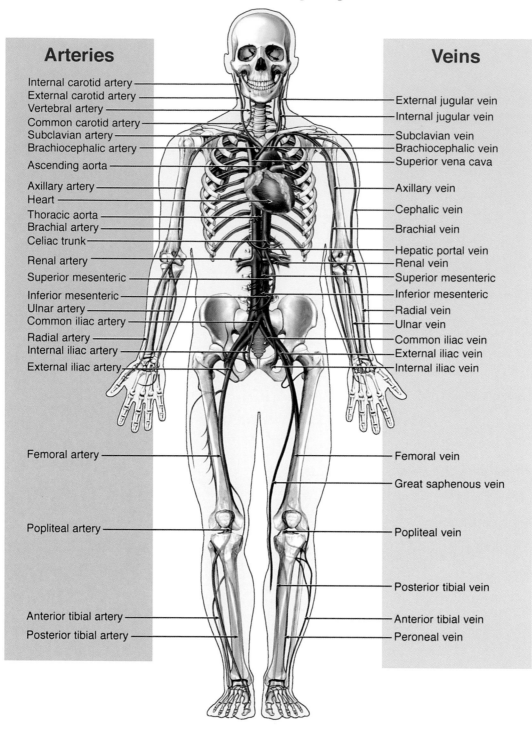

Arteries

Internal carotid artery
External carotid artery
Vertebral artery
Common carotid artery
Subclavian artery
Brachiocephalic artery
Ascending aorta
Axillary artery
Heart
Thoracic aorta
Brachial artery
Celiac trunk
Renal artery
Superior mesenteric
Inferior mesenteric
Ulnar artery
Common iliac artery
Radial artery
Internal iliac artery
External iliac artery
Femoral artery
Popliteal artery
Anterior tibial artery
Posterior tibial artery

Veins

External jugular vein
Internal jugular vein
Subclavian vein
Brachiocephalic vein
Superior vena cava
Axillary vein
Cephalic vein
Brachial vein
Hepatic portal vein
Renal vein
Superior mesenteric
Inferior mesenteric
Radial vein
Ulnar vein
Common iliac vein
External iliac vein
Internal iliac vein
Femoral vein
Great saphenous vein
Popliteal vein
Posterior tibial vein
Anterior tibial vein
Peroneal vein

Arteries and veins throughout the body have important functions. Many supply blood to specific organs or body systems.

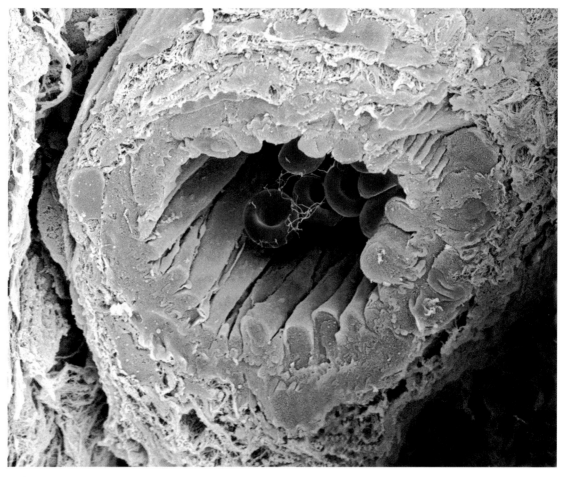

This micrograph shows red blood cells traveling through an arteriole. The thick walls of the arteriole expand and contract, which controls blood pressure.

blood to the left side of the neck, eyes, and brain. The left and right subclavian arteries deliver blood to the upper body and arms. The arteries of the descending aorta bring blood to the abdomen, digestive organs, sexual organs, and legs. These large arteries split into medium arteries that supply blood to skeletal muscles and major organs.

Arterioles, the smallest arteries, play an important role in determining blood pressure. Arterioles receive signals to increase or decrease their diameter. When they increase, or vasodilate, more blood flows through and blood pressure is reduced. When the arterioles decrease in diameter, or

MEASURING BLOOD PRESSURE

A person's blood pressure is measured by taking into account the systolic pressure, which occurs when the heart pumps, and the diastolic pressure, which is the measure between heartbeats when the heart is at rest. A normal rating for a healthy person at rest is a blood pressure of 120 over 80, which is written as 120/80. The 120 reflects the systolic measure, or the pressure of blood hitting the walls of the heart as it beats. The 80 reflects the diastolic measure, or the pressure of the heart at rest.

These numbers are expressed in milliliters of mercury, and they gauge the distance that a column of mercury rises inside a sealed cylinder. The traditional device that measures blood pressure is called a sphygmomanometer (from the Greek word, *sphygmos,* which means to pulse or throb). A sphygmomanometer is made up of an inflatable cuff connected by a tube to a rubber bulb that pumps air, and the meter, which has the mercury gauge. To check for blood pressure, a medical practitioner wraps the cuff around a person's upper arm, where a major artery lies close to the heart. The bulb is squeezed, pumping air into the cuff until the cuff has tightened and stopped the flow of blood in the arm. As the air is let out of the cuff, the practitioner uses a stethoscope to listen to the blood flowing through the artery. The practitioner records the point on the gauge or meter when the first slight thump is heard. This is the sound of blood as it starts to move through the artery. That is the systolic measure. As the cuff continues to loosen, the practitioner records the point when there is no longer a sound. This means that the blood is flowing freely, which is the diastolic measure.

Mercury sphygmomanometers and stethoscopes are used much less often today, as concerns over mercury as a toxic material have come to light. Instead, most modern medical facilities use an inflatable cuff attached to an electronic device that measure blood pressure. There are even electric devices that a person can use on his or her own. All it requires is attaching the cuff to one's arm and pressing the button on the machine. Whether or not a traditional sphygmomanometer is used, blood pressure measurements are still described in units of milliliters of mercury.

vasoconstrict, blood flow is restricted and blood pressure rises. Arterioles regulate the flow of blood and plasma through the capillaries enabling the transfer, or exchange of nutrients, oxygen, and wastes between cell walls.

In capillary exchange, the red blood cells move slowly, allowing time for nutrients and oxygen to seep out and be distributed in a process called diffusion. During diffusion, nutritional substances and oxygen pass through the spaces between the endothelial cells. The transfer is assisted by a fluid called interstitial fluid, which surrounds tissues. By the time blood reaches the capillaries, there is little pressure left to push blood along. As a result, to transfer nutrients and cell waste back and forth to the tissues, the capillaries rely on the pressure difference between the blood on the inside of the vessels and the interstitial fluid on the outside. Nutrients pass from the blood to the fluid in a process called filtration. Wastes are returned to the capillary blood in a process called reabsorption.

Once capillaries have delivered oxygen and nutrition, the carbon dioxide and other cell waste enter the capillaries and continue on to the venules. The venules are the beginning of the venous system. Venules carry the blood to larger veins which carry it back to the venae cavae and the heart, completing the systemic circuit. Returning blood is oxygen-poor and is darker, almost blue in color.

WHAT BLOOD DOES

Whole blood has several essential tasks. It delivers oxygen from the lungs to the body; it removes carbon dioxide and cell waste, returning the carbon dioxide to the lungs to be exhaled, and the cell waste to the kidneys to be filtered and passed out of the body; it transports nutrients, such as water, glucose, fats, and proteins collected from the digestive system to give energy to cells throughout the body; it carries hormones, medication, and enzymes vital for organ and tissue function and health; it clots to preserve sufficient blood volume; it delivers antibodies and fights infections; and it helps regulate body temperature.

Red Blood Cells

Red blood cells, the tiniest cells of the body, carry oxygen and remove carbon dioxide. Like other blood cells, red blood cells are created in bone marrow, which is the soft material made up of fats and other tissue found inside bones. When a red blood cell matures and leaves the marrow to enter the blood stream, it expels its nucleus (or control center) and fills the space with the iron-rich protein hemoglobin. One third of each red blood cell is made of hemoglobin.

Typically, a normal cell has a nucleus that directs its activity and causes the cell to reproduce by splitting in two. But because a mature red blood cell has rid itself of its nucleus before it enters the blood stream, it is unable to divide. Red blood cells live for just four months before wearing out. Once they die, the cells break up and are carried by the blood to the spleen, where they are discarded. Iron from the discarded hemoglobin is stored in the liver. Blood passing through the liver will carry the iron to the marrow to help in the production of more red blood cells. Nearly two million red blood cells die every second, leaving behind a constant need for fresh cells. Whenever the red blood cell numbers drop, the kidneys and liver sense a lower oxygen level and secrete a hormone called erythropoietin. This hormone stimulates production of more red blood cells in the marrow.

All red blood cells begin in the marrow as stem cells, or hematopoietic cells. A stem cell is an immature cell that can grow into any type of cell. A hematopoietic stem cell can grow into any type of blood cell. In infants, nearly all bone marrow can produce hematopoietic stem cells to make blood. But as bodies mature, adults form stem cells only in the marrow of the spine, sternum, ribs, pelvis and parts of the arms and legs. Each day, more than 250 billion new red blood cells are made in the marrow.

White Blood Cells

White blood cells, or leukocytes, travel in the plasma,
along the vessel walls. Like
red blood cells, leukocytes are
formed in the bone marrow.
But white blood cells possess
nuclei, and have a very different function. Leukocytes are
the body's defenders. There
are two basic groups: granulocytes and agranulocytes.

When studied under a mi-
croscope, one can see that
granulocytes contain small
granules or bumps. The three
types of granulocytes are neu-

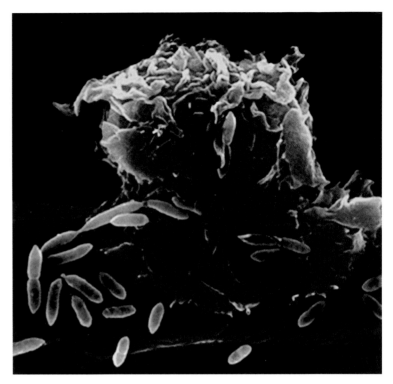

This macrophage—a type of white blood cell—is attacking
E. coli *bacteria (yellow) in the linings of the lungs. The macrophage must destroy the bacteria in order to prevent illness.*

trophils, eosinophils, and basophils. The most numerous are neutrophils,
which travel in the blood stream until they encounter a bacterial infection. Then neutrophils leave the blood and trap the bacteria by encasing it
within a membrane and attacking it with powerful enzymes. Neutrophils
are the earliest of the body's defenses and perform with such great force
that they do not live more than a few days. Eosinophils release toxic proteins carried in their granules to destroy invading parasites. Eosinophils
also help in attacking foreign bodies, or allergens, in the body. Basophils
are the rarest white blood cells, but are critical in releasing histamine, an
important protein that helps attack allergens.

The two types of agranulocytes are lymphocytes and monocytes.
Lymphocytes attack viruses and other harmful organisms and also retain
a "memory" of the foreign substance. When the body is attacked again, the

white blood cells and other parts of the immune system can defend itself faster because it remembers the invaders and how to fight them. Monocytes are large white blood cells that enter infected tissue and ingest or destroy it. Once the monocytes enter the cell, they mature into macrophages, a Greek phrase, meaning "big eaters." They are related to neutrophils, but live longer.

Platelets

With only a little more than 1 gallon (4 liters) of blood in the body, every drop is precious. When a wound occurs, the body cannot afford to lose a lot of blood. Colorless, oval-shaped cells in the blood called thrombocytes, or platelets, help prevent this. They create strands that dry and harden to form a web-like mass, or clot. They also secrete a hormone, serotonin, which constricts the blood vessels to reduce blood flow. Platelets, which are also formed in the marrow, live for just a few days in the blood. They flow along the smooth inner surfaces of blood vessels, and when they sense a tear in a vessel or an opening in the skin, they immediately affix themselves to

Fibrins (red strands) created by platelets trap red blood cells (orange) and aid in the clotting process.

the area and begin breaking apart. With the help of vitamins and other clotting substances in the blood, the broken platelets form a clot and plug up the opening. On the surface of the skin the clot is recognizable as a scab. Internally, a clot can sometimes be seen as a purplish colored bruise, or "black-and-blue" mark.

Plasma

Plasma is about 90 percent water. The rest of the plasma is composed of vital substances that energize and heal cells. These substances include sugars, salts, fatty acids, hormones, enzymes, vitamins, minerals, medications, and amino acids (protein building blocks). Blood plasma performs many tasks. It helps maintain blood pressure and it keeps blood vessels full, which prevents capillaries from collapsing and starving tissues. Other functions include regulating body temperature by carrying heat; transporting clotting material; delivering waste products to the spleen, liver, sweat glands, and kidneys; and fighting infections.

Plasma carries important proteins that originate in the liver. These are albumins, globulins, and fibrinogen. Albumins and other proteins help maintain a balance of water pressure inside blood vessels and out. The pressure, called osmotic pressure, assists in the exchange of fluids in the capillaries. Albumins transport fatty acids used for energy and hormones, such as insulin, serotonin, and adrenaline, that are necessary for organ function. The three types of globulins are alpha, beta, and gamma. Gamma globulins fight disease by forming antibodies that attack foreign substances. Alpha and beta globulins help transport iron, necessary proteins, and fats to tissue cells. Fibrinogen is a protein used by platelets to help clot blood.

Plasma helps control body temperature. When the body becomes over-heated, either through external conditions or from heat produced by the muscles during exercise, vessels dilate, or open, and bring the plasma closer

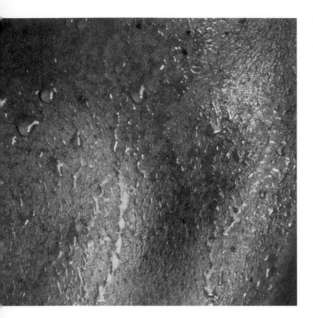

When you are overheated, blood rushes to the surface of your skin and you blush or flush. This redness—and the sweat that sometimes go along with it—is your body's way of releasing heat.

to the skin's surface. If the vessels dilate wide enough, fluids will leak through the capillaries and create sweat on the skin. Cooling air passes over the skin and lowers the temperature of the blood flowing beneath the skin's surface. The cooled blood circulates, lowering the body's temperature. In the opposite instance, when the body is chilled, vessels constrict. This slows, or stops blood flow to the skin and the body's extremities, such as the fingers, toes, and nose. This means that more warm blood is delivered to vital organs, such as the heart and the brain.

FUNCTIONS

Doctors examine the heart and monitor its functions by using several types of diagnostic tests. Besides the sphygmomanometer, other commonly used procedures include X rays, blood tests, electrocardiograms (ECG or EKG), echocardiograms, cardiac catheterization, computed tomography (CT scan), positron emission tomography (PET scan), cardiac magnetic resonance imaging (cardiac MRI), heart biopsy, and various stress tests. These kinds of tools can provide a wealth of information about the heart.

Blood tests and X rays are usually the first procedures performed. Blood tests take a laboratory sample of the blood and examine it for irregularities. X rays take a picture of the outline of the heart and are able to show any irregular shape or size. A CT scan gives a more detailed image.

A cardiac catheterization is a procedure used to detect whether arteries are blocked or are becoming too narrow. A long thin tube—the catheter—is threaded through a major artery, such as those found in the arm or legs. Then the catheter, is guided to the heart, where it releases either a dye or an electrical signal. The dye or the signal is read by a special X-ray device. The resulting image shows doctors if there are problems in the heart.

A catheter is also used to perform a biopsy. In a biopsy, the end of the catheter has a needle that scrapes a sample of heart tissue cells. These cells are then examined under a microscope or undergo other tests. Doctors use biopsies to look for diseases, such as cardiomyopathy.

An echocardiogram, also known as an ultrasound, provides a moving picture of the heart. This device sends out sound waves that bounce (or echo) off the heart and are then recorded. The echocardiogram shows the motion of the heart as it beats, pointing out any irregularities or abnormal movement. An electrocardiogram (EKG) is another method of recording the movement of the heart. An EKG uses electrodes attached to the patient's skin. The electrodes sense the electric impulses given off by the cells in the SA node as they travel through the heart. The electrodes then send the information back to a device that records the patterns on a graph. An EKG can show a person's heart rhythm, blood flow, or problems with the heart's valves or chambers.

During a PET scan of the heart, a radioactive substance is injected into the patient's blood stream. The substance gathers in concentrations around the areas of the heart and blood vessels where damage has occurred. The scan detects the radioactivity and computers process the information to create an image that a doctor can see.

A cardiac MRI is a painless procedure that uses no radiation. When a patient undergoes an MRI of the heart, he or she lies inside machine that resembles a large tube. The device uses magnetic forces to create a 3-D image of the heart. Doctors use this image to diagnose diseases or problems with the heart.

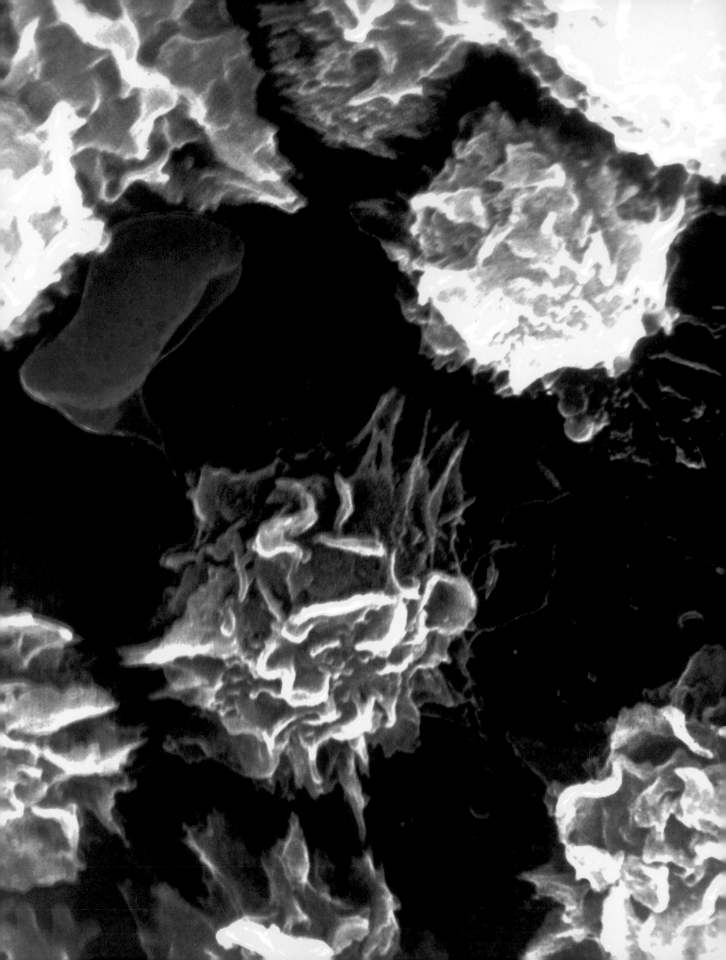

When the Circulatory System Fails

More than 70 million Americans suffer from a disease or disorder of the heart, vascular system, or blood. Cardiovascular disease is the leading cause of death in the United States. Each of the three main elements of the circulatory system—the heart, vessels, and blood—can deteriorate or fail due to unhealthy habits, genetic defects, injury, infection, or various other risk factors. Many of these risk factors are still unidentified.

Hairy cell leukemia—which gets its name from the way the leukemia cells look—is a serious blood disease that affects many people around the world.

HEART DISEASE

There are two types of heart disease: acquired and congenital. Congenital heart disorders are those that exist at birth, and acquired disorders are those that develop later in life.

Congenital Heart Disorders

Very often, congenital heart disease is apparent within two years of birth. However, sometimes the disease is not discovered until adulthood. About 1 percent of children born in the United States have congenital heart disease. Congenital heart disease, or congenital heart defect, occurs when the heart and blood vessels close to the heart do not develop normally before birth. In some instances, the disorder is mild and the infant grows up healthy. Some cases need treatment later in life. The most serious congenital disorders, however, require immediate medical attention in the form of drug therapy or surgery.

Many congenital heart defects are genetic, meaning that they are inherited traits from parents or grandparents. Other congenital defects can be caused by something that the mother experiences before the infant is born, such as having rubella (German measles) or diabetes. Defects can also occur if a pregnant woman takes certain medication, or abuses alcohol, tobacco, or drugs. However, in most cases of congenital heart defects, the causes remain unknown.

The most common congenital heart disease in a newborn is a hole in the septum. This hole causes the oxygen-rich blood to mix with the oxygen-poor blood. The hole can occur between the ventricles—the condition is called ventricular septal defect—or between the atria, which is called atrial septal defect. In each case, the stronger left side forces too much blood into the right side. This puts too much pressure on the pulmonary circuit and the lungs. As a result, babies with these defects will have a

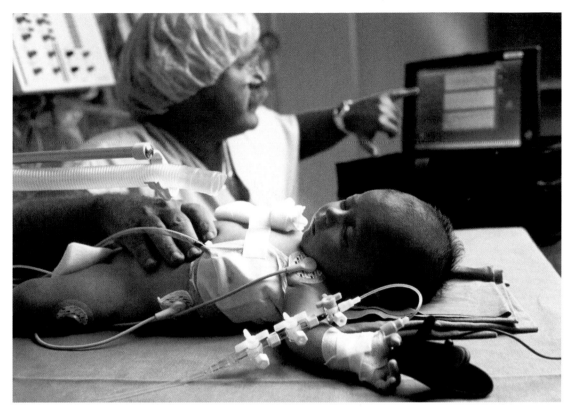

Babies who undergo heart surgery need to be closely monitored to make sure their young hearts are working correctly.

hard time breathing. The hole may close on its own, but sometimes it is necessary to perform surgery to seal the opening.

Another congenital defect, patent ductus arteriosus, occurs most often in babies born prematurely, or too early. Before birth, there is a temporary blood vessel that carries blood from the heart to the aorta, bypassing the pulmonary circuit to the lungs. After birth, this vessel is no longer needed and it naturally closes up. In infants with patent ductus arteriosus, blood continues to flow through this vessel. This mixes oxygen-poor blood with oxygen-rich blood in the aorta. The vessel must be closed through surgery.

With these and other congenital heart defects, cyanosis often occurs. Cyanosis is a condition where too little oxygen-rich blood circulates.

While oxygen-poor blood is not blue in color, it is not as bright red as oxygenated blood. This causes lips, fingers, and toes to appear blue.

Other congenital heart defects involve obstructions to blood flow, such as malformations of the tissues or muscles of the heart. Arteries or valves may also be narrowed, or stenosed. *Stenosis* is a term that refers to the narrowing of valves or arteries. When stenosis occurs, the heart strains to pump blood. Sometimes stenosis in the valves of the heart is so severe that valves are fused closed and must be surgically corrected. The aorta can also develop stenosis in a condition called coarctation of the aorta.

Acquired Heart Disorders

Acquired heart diseases often occur in adulthood, although young people can also develop one of the many disorders. Four of the most common acquired heart diseases in young people are Kawasaki disease, cardiomyopathy, rheumatic heart disease, and myocarditis. Symptoms of Kawasaki disease include an inflammation of blood vessels, a high fever, and skin rashes. Doctors treat the disease with transfusions of gamma globulin, the protein in plasma that produces antibodies. After a patient has recovered from the fever, however, he or she may have permanent damage to their coronary arteries. This damage can be treated with medication, or in more severe cases, with surgery.

Cardiomyopathy is a disease that damages the heart muscles, causing them to tighten, thicken, or become too large. Viral infections are usually the cause, with symptoms such as dizziness, swollen hands or feet, extreme tiredness, and feeling out of breath. The disease is sometimes treated with medication or with an electronic device called a pacemaker. A pacemaker is a small, battery operated disk that generates a regular pulse. Inserted under the skin, the pacemaker is attached to wires that lead to the heart. In the most severe and rare cases of cardiomyopathy, the patient may have surgery, or possibly a heart transplant.

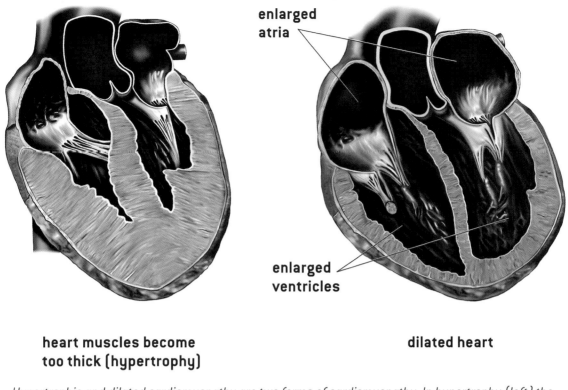

enlarged atria

enlarged ventricles

heart muscles become too thick (hypertrophy)

dilated heart

Hypertrophic and dilated cardiomyopathy are two forms of cardiomyopathy. In hypertrophy (left) the heart muscles become too thick, which makes it hard for enough blood to be pumped in and out of the heart. A heart affected by dilated cardiomyopathy (right) has enlarged, or dilated, chambers. The muscles in the walls of the chambers are too thin and cannot efficiently pump blood.

Myocarditis is caused by the body's immune system. The immune system responds to a virus or other infection, but also attacks the heart muscles. Myocarditis symptoms include cold hands and feet, decreased urine due to kidney damage, chest pain, fevers, or swelling. Damage to the heart includes scarring, an inability to pump properly, heart attacks, or an uneven heartbeat. Some of the infections that lead to myocarditis are the flu, rubella, human immunodeficiency virus (HIV), rheumatic fever, and diphtheria. There is no cure for myocarditis, though many with the disease are able to live somewhat normally. Treatments include blood pressure medication, transfusions of gamma globulins, and rest.

Rheumatic heart disease is the most common acquired heart disease that affects children. It occurs after a person has had an illness due to an infection of streptococcal bacteria, such as rheumatic fever, scarlet fever, some forms of pneumonia, or strep throat. Antibiotics will generally fight the streptococcal infection, but rheumatic heart disease can occur later after the initial infection. This causes damage to heart valves and overall fatigue or extreme tiredness. When the heart valves have been severely scarred, they may be surgically repaired or replaced.

Acquired heart disease is more common in adults than children, and the risks of acquiring the diseases increase with age. Four main categories of heart disease are coronary artery disease (CAD), heart-muscle damage, rhythm disorders, and valve abnormalities.

Coronary artery disease, or CAD, is the most common. (It is sometimes known as coronary heart disease, or CHD.) It accounts for more than 70 percent of all deaths from heart disease each year. A person with CAD has atherosclerosis in the coronary arteries. In atherosclerosis, plaque—

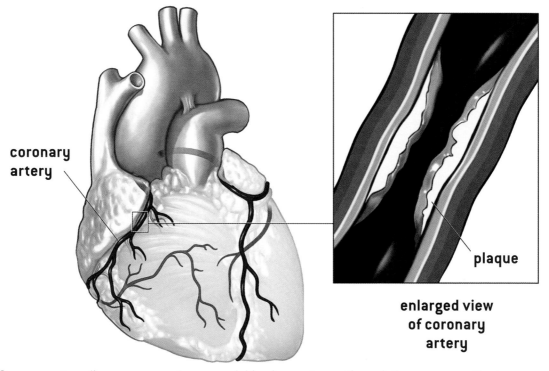

coronary
artery

plaque

enlarged view
of coronary
artery

Coronary artery disease occurs when enough blood cannot pass through the coronary arties because of a build up of plaque on the vessel walls.

which is a collection of calcium, fats, and cell waste deposits—builds up on the inner walls of large arteries. The deposits mostly come from cholesterol, a soft, fat-like substance that is necessary for making some hormones and building cell membranes. The body makes cholesterol in the liver, but it also absorbs extra cholesterol directly from foods such as egg yolks, meat, and whole-milk dairy products. Cholesterol cannot move through the body without the help of substances in the body called lipoproteins. High-density lipoproteins (HDL) carry the cholesterol out of the blood stream and to the liver, where it can be expelled from the body. (HDL is often called "good cholesterol.") Low-density lipoproteins (LDL) carry the cholesterol through the blood to the cells. (LDL is considered the bad, or harmful, cholesterol.) When there is more cholesterol than the body needs, the LDL builds up along the inner walls of the arteries, creating layers of plaque, and restricting the flow of blood. As the coronary arteries narrow from plaque build-up, the heart becomes starved for blood and oxygen. Heart cells begin to die, causing chest pain, or angina. Symptoms of CAD are pains in the chest, back, or arm, shortness of breath, dizziness, and palpitations, which are feelings that the heart is beating rapidly and hard.

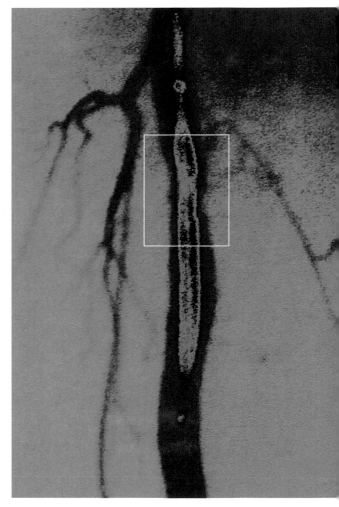

During this angioplasty procedure, doctors inserted a tiny balloon that will widen the blood vessel and allow blood to flow through.

Treatment for CAD varies. For some people, medication and a change of diet provide relief. Others may undergo a procedure called angioplasty. In this procedure, a tiny balloon attached to the end of a catheter is inserted into the clogged artery. When the balloon expands, it breaks up the plaque and opens the pathway. If the blockage is too hardened for a balloon, other catheter procedures are used. These include laser angioplasty, which burns the plaque away, and atherectomy, which uses a surgical drill to cut through the plaque.

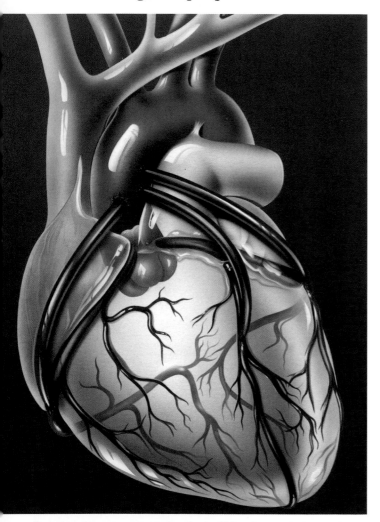

Coronary bypass uses transplanted blood vessels to create a new pathway from the coronary arteries to the aorta. When three arteries are used to go around three blockages, the surgery is called a triple bypass.

Coronary artery bypass surgery is a more involved treatment for CAD. When the disease becomes life-threatening and less invasive treatments have not helped, surgeons perform this bypass. A blood vessel is taken from a different part of the body—usually a large vein from the leg. This vessel is used to connect the aorta to a part of the damaged coronary artery beyond the clogged area. Blood flows through this vessel, bypassing the blockage.

Sometimes the plaque along the coronary artery walls bursts apart, causing platelets in the blood to form a large clot that halts blood flow. When the heart's blood supply is interrupted in this way, the heart experiences a myocardial infarction, or a heart attack. During a heart attack, a person's symptoms may be angina, dizziness, shortness of breath, extreme tiredness, irregular heartbeats, and a choking sensation. If the blood stoppage lasts for more than a few minutes, heart muscle becomes permanently damaged and cells die. Heart attacks can be fatal. However, many people survive them, but with damage to their hearts. The amount of muscle that is destroyed depends on the size of the area that the affected coronary artery supplies with blood. Damaged muscles will form scar tissue after an attack, stiffening the heart and preventing it from pumping normally. After or during a heart attack, it is essential that a person seeks medical assistance as soon as possible. Drug treatments include medication that will thin the blood, restore normal heart rhythms, break up the clot, or prevent new clots from forming. Additional oxygen is given, and sometimes an emergency bypass operation is performed.

Some heart diseases are caused by irregular heartbeats and flawed electrical signals. If the heart beats too fast, too slow, or inconsistently, blood flow is disturbed. A normal heartbeat consists of an electrical impulse that begins in the SA node of the heart and travels to the AV node. When any change occurs in this pattern, the heart experiences arrhythmia, or abnormal heart rhythms. Some arrhythmias are mild and brief. Those that are not can cause dangerous changes in the heart rate or rhythm. Arrhythmia varies from person to person. Doctors usually diagnose the severity of the condition using EKGs. Some people are treated with medication, pacemakers, or diet changes. Some require surgery, CPR, or electric shock to restore normal heartbeat.

Bradycardia is the term for a slowed heart rate. It can be caused by coronary heart disease or by medication that slows the signal from the SA node to the AV node. Sometimes the slowed heart beat does not pass at all from the upper chambers to the lower chambers. Another part of the heart provides a "back-up" impulse. When the heart beats too slowly to effectively circulate blood, a pacemaker is usually inserted. A pacemaker

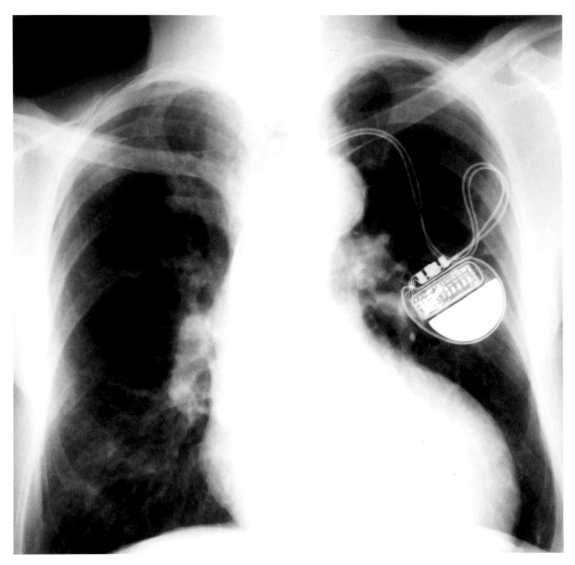

An X ray shows a pacemaker positioned near this person's heart. Wires from the device lead to the heart and help control the electric impulses needed to make the heart muscle work.

can keep a heart pumping regularly for eight to ten years before the device needs to be replaced.

For people with tachycardia, the heart beats too fast. Rapid heartbeats can occur in either the atria or the ventricles. If it occurs in the atria, the heart is unable to pump correctly and a person may feel heart palpitations, dizziness, and a fainting sensation. When the ventricles beat too fast, the heart is in danger of fibrillating. Fibrillation is a term for an uncontrollable fluttering of the heart muscle. When the heart fibrillates, it is unable to pump blood at all. Organs are deprived of oxygen, and without immediate correction, the heart can go into sudden cardiac arrest. Sudden cardiac arrest is different from a heart attack and is likely to be fatal without immediate medical attention. To restore normal heart beat and stop a heart from fibrillating, the patient will need an electric shock given by a device called a defibrillator and possibly CPR (cardio pulmonary resuscitation, which is a combination of chest compressions and assisted breathing).

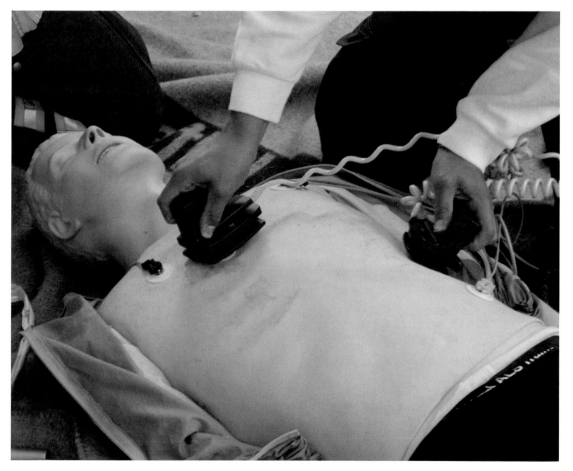

Emergency medical technicians (EMTs) who respond to medical emergencies learn how to use defibrillators on a practice dummy. The defibrillator paddles are put on the chest so that the electrical current can travel to the heart.

HEART VALVE DISEASE

Heart valve disease diminishes the ability of the heart to circulate blood. Young people can develop the disease, but more often the disease appears in older people. There are four valves—two that allow blood to enter the ventricles, and two that let blood flow out. Valves can leak, called regurgitation, or fail to open and close completely, called stenosis. Sometimes they can fail in both ways. Doctors can detect stenosis or regurgitation by listening to the heart with a stethoscope, or testing with an echocardiogram. The sound of a healthy heart is often described as *lubb-dubb*. The *lubb* is the sound of the atrial valves closing, and *dubb* is the sound of the ventricular valves closing.

Sometimes, there is an extra sound, a *shh* sound between the *lubb* and *dubb*. This extra sound is called a heart murmur. Most murmurs are not a cause for alarm, and many children and young adults have them for brief periods. Yet the sound could indicate a heart valve problem. Doctors can repair a damaged valve with medication, with surgery, or catheterization to stretch the narrowed valve. If the damage is severe, the valve can be surgically replaced either with a mechanical valve or by using the heart valve of a pig. Mechanical valves are long-lasting, but they attract platelets that can form dangerous blood clots. People with a mechanical valve replacement must take anti-clotting medication throughout their lives. Pig valves do not cause blood clots generally, but they do not last as long.

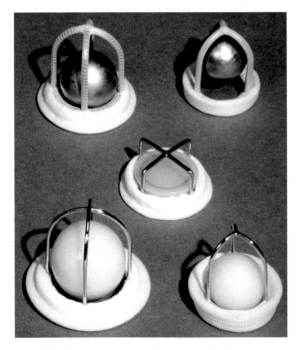

Artificial heart valves can be made of plastic or metal. The valves differ in size and function, depending upon where they are being placed.

A surgeon holds an artificial heart in her hands. Made of plastic, metal, and other materials, this heart has chambers and valves that are supposed to function like those in a regular heart.

HEART TRANSPLANTS

After other therapies have failed, there are times when heart disease is so severe that there is no other alternative to saving a person's life than to remove the damaged heart and replace it with a healthy heart. A healthy heart must come from an organ donor who has recently suffered brain death. The donor heart is kept pumping by artificial means until it can be removed and transported to a waiting recipient. There were more than 2,000 heart transplants performed in the United States in recent years.

About 4,000 people are on a national waiting list for donor hearts. However, not everyone waiting for a heart transplant lives to receive one. To be selected for the waiting list, a candidate must be an otherwise healthy person. The heart donor and heart recipient must be within four to six hours transportation time from one another. The blood types and other tissues must also be a close match.

On December 3, 1967, South African doctor Christiaan Barnard performed the world's first human-to-human heart transplant surgery. The patient lived for eighteen days after the surgery. However, on January 6, 1968, Dr. Norman Shumway performed the first heart transplant in the United States. In the years following, doctors strove to make transplants more successful. Today, heart transplant recipients have an 85 percent chance of surviving one year after surgery, and a 70 percent chance of living five years after surgery. There are patients alive today who have lived a virtually normal life for more than twenty years after their transplants.

When a heart transplant is performed, the heart, after removal from the donor, cannot stay healthy and usable for longer than four to six hours. As a result, it is hurriedly transported to the heart recipient's hospital. Meanwhile, the recipient is hooked up to a heart lung bypass device that will pump oxygenated blood throughout the patient's body while the old heart is removed and the new one is transplanted. The entire procedure takes approximately four to six hours. Hospital recovery time, once several months long, can now be a one-week stay.

The greatest challenge to recovery is the patient's immune system. It will naturally respond to the donated heart as if it were an unwanted foreign invader. The immune system will try to attack and destroy the new heart. Special medications help prevent the recipient from rejecting the donor heart. There are many side effects that arise from these anti-rejection medications, but many recent advances have helped improve the patient's health and quality of life.

VASCULAR DISEASES

Disorders of the Arteries

Arteriosclerosis is a general term for diseases of the arteries. The word comes from the Greek *arterio*, which means artery, and *sclerosis*, which means hardening or scarring. There are three types of arteriosclerosis: atherosclerosis, arteriolosclerosis, and Monckeberg's arteriosclerosis.

The most common form of arteriosclerosis is atherosclerosis. Atherosclerosis is a build up of plaque in the arteries that deliver blood to the brain, vital organs, and limbs. It develops over time as the smooth inner walls of the vessels become inflamed, infected, or otherwise damaged. White blood cells collect in the damaged lining. The white blood cells attract fatty deposits such as cholesterol, body wastes, and calcium. Together they form the plaque that hardens and thickens the inner lining, narrowing the passageway for blood. As in coronary artery disease, body tissues starve because they lack oxygen and nutrients. Frequently, atherosclerosis develops in the carotid arteries. If these arteries to the brain are blocked, a stroke can result. This deprives the brain of oxygen and kills brain cells. A stroke often leads to loss of speech, memory, or some form of paralysis, or problems moving. Along with coronary artery disease, strokes are the leading causes of illness and death in the United States.

Arteriolosclerosis is a hardening and narrowing of the arterioles, and it usually affects the blood supply to the kidneys. When the arterioles thicken with cholesterol and blood flow is restricted, the kidneys are no longer able to perform their function of filtering excess fluid and waste from the blood. Mönckeberg's arteriosclerosis is a stiffening, but not a narrowing, of the medium-size arteries, and is generally not a serious illness.

Venous Disorders

There are two basic types of veins: superficial, which are found just

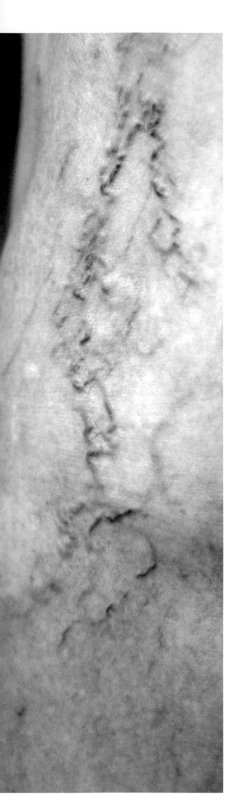

under the skin, and deep veins, which occur further from the surface. Large veins in the legs are embedded in muscles. Veins in the legs are the most susceptible to vascular disease due to the force of gravity, which pulls blood downward, and the effort required by muscles and valves in the veins to deliver blood back to the heart. Some of the diseases that affect veins are varicose veins, phlebitis, deep vein thrombosis, and venous insufficiency.

Varicose veins are a common disease of the superficial veins in the legs. When veins become weakened or dilated, blood does not flow up toward the heart. Instead, it pools against valves in the veins. As a result, the veins become large and show through the skin. The condition can be painful, but is not generally very serious. There are several steps that can be taken to reduce the discomfort. These include not standing for long periods, resting with the legs elevated, walking around to improve blood flow in the legs, and wearing special elastic stockings that squeeze the legs and encourage blood flow.

Phlebitis is a blood clot that has formed in superficial veins, causing the veins to swell, redden, and become painful. Bandages and medication often correct the problem.

Deep vein thrombosis is a much more serious blood clot that occurs in the deep veins. This type of blood clot not only causes serious pain and swelling,

◀ *Varicose veins are noticeable on the arms or on the backs of a person's legs.*

but it can be potentially fatal if it breaks away and enters the blood stream, where it may lodge in the heart or lungs. Medication can help thin the blood and prevent further clotting.

Venous insufficiency is a breakdown of the system of veins. When the leg veins have become weakened and dilated and blood pressure in them is too high, poor circulation results. This leads to swelling, pain, and wounds that develop near the ankle. These wounds do not heal quickly, and are called venous skin ulcers. Treatment can include medication, surgery, and the basic precautions used to correct varicose veins.

HIGH BLOOD PRESSURE

When blood is pumped from the heart, it pushes with great force against the walls of the arteries. The pressure is needed to ensure that blood reaches all the capillaries throughout the body. Yet if the pressure is too much, it will cause hypertension, or high blood pressure. There is no single direct cause of high blood pressure, but there are many risk factors that can contribute to the disease. These include smoking, abusing drugs or alcohol, diabetes, kidney disease, lack of exercise, too much salt in the diet, and being overweight. Many diseases of the circulatory system are caused in part by high blood pressure, and nearly 25 percent of all Americans over the age of eighteen have the condition. Though it is a serious disease, most people feel no symptoms from high blood pressure. But it can lead to heart attack, heart failure, and stroke. Hypertension can also damage the blood vessels, brain, and other vital organs.

When vessels thicken with plaque, the blood is forced through very narrow channels and the pressure increases, weakening the artery walls, causing an aneurysm. An aneurysm is a serious condition in which the weakened artery begins to bulge and pressure on the bulge causes it to burst. This is an urgent medical situation, especially if the aneurysm

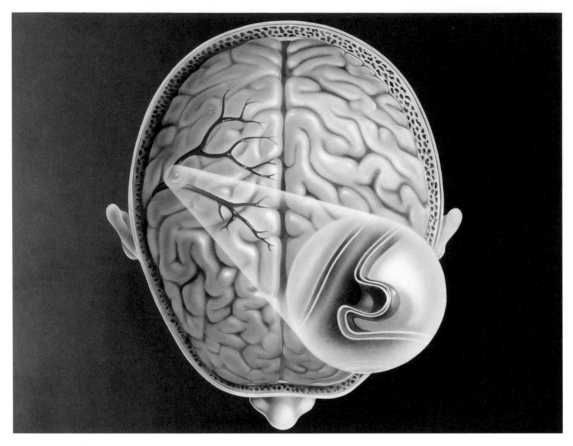

The bulge that is forming on this blood vessel in the brain is called a cerebral aneurysm. If left untreated, this aneurysm can cause brain damage or death.

occurs in the brain. Uncontrolled bleeding in the brain is another type of stroke. Treatment includes medication and surgery. Medication, a healthy diet, and exercise can help manage high blood pressure, but there is no cure.

Low blood pressure, or hypotension, is a less commonly occurring disorder. Many athletes have lower than normal blood pressure, which is a sign of health and not illness. Yet hypotension can be a cause for concern if low pressure prevents blood from flowing completely around its circuit. Low blood pressure can develop due to severe dehydration, a sudden loss of blood, severe infection, allergic reaction, heart valve problems, heart and allergy medication, or a slowed heart beat.

BLOOD DISORDERS

Blood disorders can be either genetic or acquired. Red blood cells, white blood cells, platelets, and blood proteins can be affected. There are several types of anemia, which are diseases of the red blood cells. Persons with anemia have too few red blood cells, reducing the amount of oxygen and nutrients to cells. A person with anemia suffers from pain, fatigue, and stress on vital organs. Some forms of anemia are inherited, such as sickle-cell anemia. Some are acquired, such as iron-deficiency anemia.

Sickle-cell anemia is a disease most often suffered by people of African, Mediterranean, or Middle Eastern descent. In sickle-cell anemia, the red blood cells have an abnormal shape. They are long and curved, rather than round, resembling a tool called a sickle. This abnormal shape causes the cells to become snagged in arteries. Sometimes sickle cells can completely block arteries. Sickle cells also carry a different type of hemoglobin that transports less oxygen to cells. There is no cure, but treatments include rest, blood transfusions, vitamins, antibiotics, and pain medication. Scientists have recently discovered that people with sickle cells are more resistant to the mosquito-borne, life-threatening disease malaria, which occurs in Africa, the Mediterranean region, and the Middle East.

The most common form of anemia that develops in young people is iron-deficiency anemia. Iron-deficiency anemia occurs when there is not enough iron in the diet or when the body is unable to absorb iron. Iron is a mineral necessary for the production of hemoglobin. Without hemoglobin red blood cells do not survive. Symptoms include jaundice (a yellowish cast to skin and whites of eyes due to an excess of dead red blood cells in the liver), fatigue, and dizziness. If the iron-deficiency anemia is not treated, children can suffer from developmental problems. Treatment includes taking iron or vitamins such as B12 and folic acid, antibiotics, and other medication that helps the production of red blood cells.

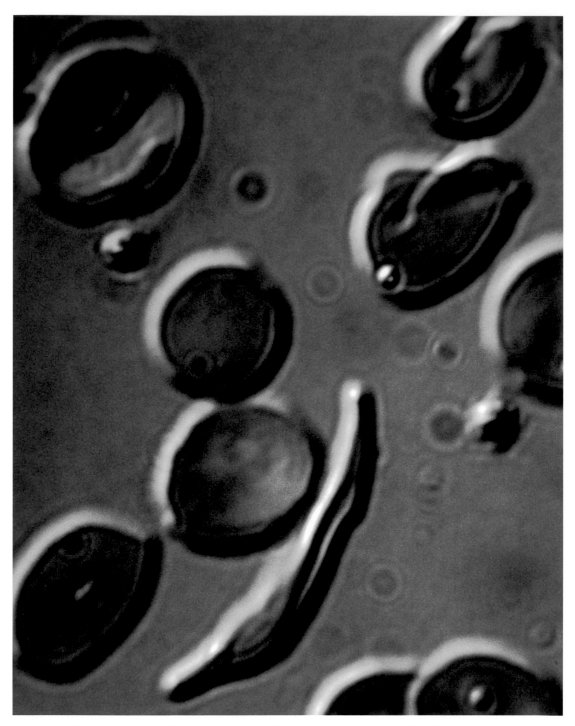

A person with sickle cell anemia has red blood cells that are not round and flat. The elongated shape makes it harder for the red blood cells—and the oxygen and nutrients they carry—to travel through the body.

When too few white blood cells are formed in the marrow, the body is unable to fight infections, and immune diseases develop. Sometimes, too many white blood cells form. This crowds out the red blood cells, and leads to a disease known as leukemia. Leukemia, or cancer of the blood, is not an inherited disease. It develops after birth and must be treated with strong drugs that kill the abnormal white blood cells, and help form more red blood cells. In serious cases, doctors use cancer therapies such as radiation and chemotherapy to kill the patient's bone marrow. The old bone marrow is replaced with marrow from a healthy donor with a matching blood type. Leukemia can be fatal, but some types of leukemia are managed or cured.

Platelets and other clotting substances in the blood can also fail to function normally. Thrombocytopenia is a disease that results from too few platelets. A person with the disease bruises and bleeds easily. The disease is acquired, sometimes as a result of infections, leukemia, or certain medications. Hemophilia is a genetic disease passed from the mother to the child. Nearly all people with hemophilia are male. People with hemophilia are missing certain clotting substances in their plasma, and are unable to stop bleeding. Uncontrollable bleeding inside the body can damage vital organs. Hemophilia is treated with blood transfusions and medication. The most common bleeding disorder, von Willebrand disease, is also inherited and affects both males and females. It is not as severe as hemophilia, and can be controlled by medication.

4

Staying Healthy

Powerful and efficient, the circulatory system works faithfully to supply blood throughout the body. Yet the network of blood vessels, heart, and blood requires care and attention in order to stay healthy. Although cardiovascular disease is not a major cause of death in young people, it is the leading cause of death in adults. Many behaviors and unhealthy life style patterns that contribute to cardiovascular disease can develop early in life. The unhealthy habits formed when you are a child can continue when you are an adult, leading to health problems. Young people who know the risks—as well as how to manage or prevent heart and vascular disease—can lower their chances of developing these diseases later in life.

A healthy diet filled with the right amount of fresh fruits and vegetables helps to keep your body in shape.

RISK FACTORS

There are two types of risk factors for heart disease—those that can be controlled, and those over which there is no control. A risk factor is a condition or behavior that adds to the chance of developing a certain disease. In heart disease and other disorders of the circulatory system, there are a few uncontrollable factors, such as genetics, age, race, and gender. A person who has a congenital or an inherited disease or has a family history of heart disease has a greater risk of developing cardiovascular disease. As people get older, their risk also increases. African Americans, Mexican Americans, and Native Americans have a greater tendency toward heart disease than other groups. Men are more likely than women to experience a heart attack, although women over the age of fifty-five have an equal risk of developing heart disease as men. Knowing these risks, it

Junk food like potato chips have been fried in fats and oils that are bad for your heart and for your general health.

is important for people who have one or more uncontrollable risk factors to avoid or manage the risk factors they can control.

Risk factors that can be controlled, prevented, or managed include a poor diet, being overweight, lack of exercise, high blood pressure, uncontrolled diabetes, smoking, high cholesterol, and constant stress and anger. A poor diet and being overweight are serious but avoidable risk factors for high blood pressure, high cholesterol, and cardiovascular disease. Good nutrition is critical to a healthy body. A diet rich in fruits, vegetables, and fiber and low in salt and fat is "heart-healthy." Health officials recommend eating more fish, soy protein, fruits, whole grains, beans, and vegetables. People should eat fewer fatty meats, fried foods, and sugary drinks, as well as less cheese, whole milk, butter, fat, and salt. Some fats are healthy, such as olive or canola oil, but most are not. Palm and coconut oils that are found in processed foods like potato chips and crackers are not healthy. Fats known as saturated, or trans, fats that are

Nutrition Facts

Serving Size 1 Cake (43g)
Servings Per Container 5

Amount Per Serving

Calories 200 Calories from Fat 90

	% Daily Value*
Total Fat 10g	15%
Saturated Fat 5g	25%
Trans Fat 0g	
Cholesterol 0mg	0%
Sodium 100mg	4%
Total Carbohydrate 26g	9%
Dietary Fiber 0g	0%
Sugars 19g	
Protein 1g	

Vitamin A 0%	•	Vitamin C 0%
Calcium 0%	•	Iron 2%

* Percent Daily Values are based on a 2,000 calorie diet. Your daily values may be higher or lower depending on your calorie needs:

	Calories:	2,000	2,500
Total Fat	Less than	65g	80g
Sat. Fat	Less than	20g	25g
Cholesterol	Less than	300mg	300mg
Sodium	Less than	2,400mg	2,400mg
Total Carbohydrate		300g	375g
Dietary Fiber		25g	30g

All manufactured food products in the United States are required to have labels that tell the consumer the ingredients and the nutritional content. Part of eating healthy includes knowing how much fat, cholesterol, sodium, and sugars you are including in your daily diet.

FOOD SUBSTITUTES FOR A HEALTHY HEART

Healthy eating habits should begin in childhood. Everyone should eat a diet low in fat, sugars, and sodium, and high in fiber, fruits, and vegetables. If you are eating prepared foods, read the label. Avoid saturated fats and trans fats, high fructose corn syrup and other refined sugars, and added salt. The U.S. Food and Drug Administration (FDA) recommends choosing these substitutes:

INSTEAD OF:	DO THIS:
whole milk, 2 percent milk, and cream	use 1 percent milk or skim milk
fried foods	eat baked, steamed, boiled, broiled, or microwaved foods
lard, butter, or palm and coconut oils	cook with unsaturated vegetable oils, such as corn, olive, canola, safflower, sesame, soybean, sunflower, or peanut
fatty cuts of meat, such as prime rib	eat lean cuts of meat or cut off the fatty parts
one whole egg in recipes	use two egg whites
sour cream and mayonnaise	use plain low-fat yogurt, low-fat cottage cheese, or low-fat or "light" sour cream
sauces, butter, and salt	season foods with herbs and spices
regular hard and processed cheeses	eat low-fat, low-sodium cheeses
salted potato chips and other salty snacks	choose low-fat, unsalted tortilla and potato chips and unsalted pretzels and popcorn

From the Department of Health and Human Services, Food and Drug Administration

MyPyramid.gov
STEPS TO A HEALTHIER YOU

Several vitamins and minerals are good for the blood and help prevent heart disease. Among them are vitamins A, C, E, B9 (folic acid), B12, and beta-carotene (which helps make Vitamin A). Iron is the main ingredient in hemoglobin, and folic acid and B12 are also needed to make red blood cells. While some people may take vitamins or mineral supplements, the best way to stay healthy is to eat fruits, vegetables, beans, nuts, whole grains, and vegetable oils. Red meat, fish, and poultry are good sources of iron, but they should be limited to 5 to 5.5 ounces each day. The food pyramid provided by the United States Department of Agriculture (http://www.mypyramid.gov) gives advice on a healthy diet and proper amounts of exercise.

Doctors and nutritionists recommend healthy snacks like granola or cereal with fresh fruit and low-fat milk.

found in foods derived from animals, such as hamburgers and ice cream, can also be bad for you if you eat too much of them.

Choosing foods carefully is the easiest way to reduce the chances of developing heart disease, high blood pressure, and becoming overweight. Read nutrition labels on packaging. Develop a lifelong pattern of enjoying healthy foods in moderation. Being aware of calories consumed and practicing reasonable portion control, or the amount eaten at each meal, is also essential. Calorie intake should be appropriate for body type and activity level. This will lead to increased energy and a healthy body weight. Your family doctor or a nutritionist can help you figure out what kinds of foods—and how much—make up a healthful diet.

Exercise and physical activity are also necessary to maintain a healthy heart and vascular system. Doctors believe that far too many people—especially young people—are sedentary, or do not get enough exercise. By sitting for long periods at computers, television, video games, at desks, or behind steering wheels, Americans have become more obese and less physically fit.

Exercise improves the muscles of the heart, lowers blood pressure and cholesterol, reduces stress, and aids in overall well-being. The exercise that a person undertakes to be healthy does not need to be vigorous. Not

HEART HEALTH IN SCHOOLS

Many people are familiar with vending machines in public schools. Very often, they dispense sugary sodas and other quick snacks known as junk food, such as candy bars, potato chips, cookies, pastries, and other processed high-fat, high-sugar foods. Around the country, doctors, health organizations, parents, and students are asking, "Why are these unhealthy foods so available?" It is widely accepted that sugary drinks and junk food add to the danger of young people becoming overweight or obese. Unhealthy weight can lead to high blood pressure, high cholesterol, and heart disease. In the United States today, nearly 25 percent of students are overweight, or are at risk of becoming overweight and developing serious health problems.

Many school districts and some state legislatures have decided to begin some heart-healthy reforms. In some states, laws declare that schools should, "contribute to the nutritional well-being of the child and aid in establishing good food habits." Many believe that it should be a school's responsibility to promote sensible nutrition for its students. In these schools, vending machines offer juice, sugar-free iced tea, water, and 1 percent milk instead of soda, high-sugar sports drinks, and whole milk. Healthy snacks found in these new vending machines include low-fat, low-salt chips and pretzels, dried fruits, low-fat whole-grain crackers, nuts, trail mix, granola, cereal, and protein bars. Through these healthy choices, it is everyone's hope that students will develop wholesome eating habits that will continue through adulthood.

The American Heart Association reports that high blood pressure, diabetes, and high cholesterol are a growing epidemic among young people. The organization recommends that schools provide healthy diet choices and encourage all young people to participate daily in physical activity. In recent years, public schools have been expected to improve their students' standardized test scores. Many health officials believe that the emphasis on testing has taken away opportunities for physical education and after-school sports. In the past twenty years, students have not only become more overweight, but the percentage of students participating in physical education classes has decreased by 20 percent. Physical inactivity is a major risk factor for cardiovascular disease. Exercising at least thirty minutes every day greatly reduces the risks of obesity and heart disease.

In order for exercise to be beneficial to your heart, you must do some sort of physical activity that makes your heart work harder than it would if you were simply standing still.

everyone needs to run a mile each day. What is more important is that a person exercises or participates in an energetic physical activity for at least thirty minutes each day. Choices may be running, swimming, cycling, playing sports, dancing, working out at the gym, or just briskly walking.

The number one risk factor in cardiovascular (and many other) diseases is smoking tobacco or being near anyone who is smoking tobacco. Smokers have more than twice the risk of non-smokers in developing heart disease, sudden cardiac death, or of dying after a heart attack. The tar, nicotine, and other chemicals in tobacco smoke drastically increase the risk that arteries will harden.

Healthy exercise does not mean that you have to go to a gym or run around a track. Taking a brisk walk is a healthy way to include exercise in your daily schedule.

Diabetes is another critical, but controllable, risk factor for developing heart disease. Seventeen million Americans have diabetes, and heart disease is the leading cause of death among them. Diabetes is, in itself, a serious disease in which the body does not produce or efficiently use insulin, a hormone needed to convert food into energy. People with diabetes should not ignore it. They must be under a physician's care to manage the disease with a special diet, exercise, or medication.

Fifty million Americans have hypertension. They are not all adults, and health officials say that the beginnings of hypertension are set at an early age. Even children as young as six can develop high blood pressure and should be tested. Poor eating habits, including too much sugar, fat, and salt, and not enough exercise, contribute to high blood pressure. Anyone, at any age, especially if they are overweight or inactive, can be at risk for thickened arteries and the plaque buildup that leads to hypertension and atherosclerosis. Hypertension has no physical symptoms, so it is very important to see a health care practitioner regularly to monitor blood pressure.

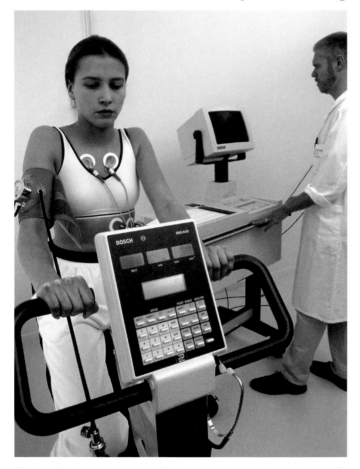

Doctors can monitor heart function through stress tests. During a stress test, a patient performs physical activity to make the heart work hard. The results of the test can help a person find out if his or her heart is functioning properly.

New medication, treatments, technology, prevention awareness, and increased understanding of how the heart and circulatory system works have helped Americans with heart or vascular disease live longer, more rewarding lives. Despite the efforts of medical professionals, heart disease is still the leading cause of death among Americans. With the right treatment, a quick response, physical therapy, and diet changes, a person who suffers a heart attack can recover and live a healthy life. However, prevention is the key to better cardiovascular health. People must take responsibility for their own risk factors, and avoid adopting the poor habits that become risk factors. While it is true that cardiovascular disease can occur without any obvious risk factors present, chances for avoiding or surviving cardiovascular disease are greatly enhanced by exercise, healthy eating, and other wholesome lifestyle habits.

People of all ages should have their blood pressure monitored regularly. Blood pressure measurements are always a part of a check up or physical with your doctor.

Glossary

aorta—The largest artery of the body, rising from the left ventricle.

aortic semilunar valve—A valve that lies between a ventricle and the aorta. It closes to prevent blood from backing up into the heart after the ventricles contract.

arrhythmia—An abnormal rhythm of the heart beat.

arteriole—A small arterial branch that delivers blood to the capillaries.

artery—A muscular blood vessel that carries blood away from the heart.

atherosclerosis—A build up of plaque in the arteries.

atrioventricular node (AV node)—The lower area in the heart that provides electrical stimulation for heart movement.

atrioventricular valve—A valve between the upper and lower chambers of the heart.

atrium—One of the upper chambers of the heart.

blood pressure—The force or pressure exerted by the heart in pumping blood, or the pressure of blood as measured in the arteries.

bradycardia—A heart rhythm that is slow.

capillary—The smallest blood vessel.

cardiac—Concerning the heart—from the Greek *kardia,* meaning "heart."

cardiovascular—Concerning the heart and blood vessels.

congenital—A condition present before or at birth.

coronary artery—An artery that supplies blood to the heart.

coronary artery disease (CAD)—Blockage of the arteries that provide blood to the heart.

diastole—The heart at rest between contractions.

endocardium—The inner layer of the heart.

epicardium—The outer layer of the heart.

erythrocyte—A red blood cell.

heart attack— A condition occurring when a section of the heart is deprived of oxygenated blood and dies.

hypertension—Also known as high blood pressure; refers to blood pressure that is consistently above the normal range.

inferior vena cava—A major vein leading to the right atrium of the heart, bringing oxygen-poor blood from the lower parts of the body.

interstitial fluid—The fluid filling the microscopic spaces between cells of the body.

leukocyte—A white blood cell.

mitral valve—The heart valve between the left atrium and left ventricle.

myocardial infarction—A heart attack.

myocardium—The thick, muscular middle layer of the heart.

pacemaker—An electrical device that is implanted under the skin and provides electrical impulses to regulate heartbeat.

pulmonary artery—An artery carrying deoxygenated blood from the heart to the lungs.

pulmonary—Concerning the lungs.

pulmonary veins—Blood vessels bringing oxygen-rich blood from the lungs to the left atrium.

regurgitation—The abnormal backward flowing of blood through a valve of the heart.

septum—A wall that divides the right and left sides of the heart.

sinoatrial node (SA node)—The upper area of the heart that initiates electrical impulses.

sphygmomanometer—A medical device that measures blood pressure.

stenosis—The narrowing or constriction of an opening, such as a heart valve.

superior vena cava—A major vein leading to the right atrium of the heart, bringing oxygen-poor blood from the upper part of the body.

systole—The heart contraction.

tachycardia—A heart rhythm that is too fast.

tricuspid valve—The atrioventricular valve between the right atrium and right ventricle.

valve—In the heart, a tissue structure that opens and closes to allow blood flow in only one direction, found between two chambers of the heart, or between a chamber of the heart and a blood vessel, or along veins in the lower body.

vascular—Concerning the blood vessels.

vein—A blood vessel that carries deoxygenated blood back to the heart.

ventricle—A lower chamber of the heart.

venule—A small venous branch that carries blood from the capillaries to a vein.

Find Out More

Books

Gold, John Coopersmith. *The Circulatory and Lymphatic Systems.* Berkeley Heights, NJ: Enslow Publishers, 2004.

Haney, Johannah. *Heart Disease.* Tarrytown, NY: Benchmark Books, 2005.

Schraff, Anne E. *Dr. Charles Drew: Blood Bank Innovator.* Berkeley Heights, NJ: Enslow Publishers, 2003.

Whittemore, Susan. *The Circulatory System.* Philadelphia: Chelsea House Publishers, 2004.

Web Sites

The American Heart Association
http://www.americanheart.org

The American Red Cross — Blood Donation
http://www.redcross.org/donate/give

The Heart and the Circulatory System — The National Health Museum
http://www.accessexcellence.org/AE/AEC/CC/heart_background.html

Heart-Health Topics – Texas Heart Institute
http://texasheart.org/HIC/Topics/index.cfm

Information and Resources for the Congenital Heart Defects Community
http://www.congenitalheartdefects.com

Introduction to Hematology (the study of blood) — Puget Sound Blood Center
http://www.psbc.org/hematology/index.htm

Bibliography

"Anatomy of the Human Circulatory System." The Biology Pages. Dr. John W. Kimball. Aug. 2003.

http://users.rcn.com/jkimball.ma.ultranet/BiologyPages/C/Circulation.html

"Blood Vessels." Encyclopedia of Nursing & Allied Health. Ed. Kristine Krapp. Gale Group, Inc., 2002. eNotes.com. 2006.

http://www.enotes.com/nursing-encyclopedia/blood-vessels

"Body Basics: Blood." Kids Health for Parents. The Nemours Foundation's Center for Children's Health Media. 1995-2007.

http://www.kidshealth.org/parent/general/body_basics/blood.html

Brawley, Robert K. *The Johns Hopkins Atlas of Human Functional Anatomy.* Baltimore, MD: Johns Hopkins University Press, 1997.

"Cardiology: Treatment." Children's Hospital of Philadelphia. 1996-2007.

http://www.chop.edu/consumer/jsp/division/generic.jsp?id=75559

"Circulation." 2006;113:e85-e151. American Heart Association, Inc. 2006.

http://circ.ahajournals.org/cgi/content/full/113/6/e85#SEC3

"The Circulatory System." The Biology Web. Clinton Community College, State University of New York.

http://faculty.clinton.edu/faculty/Michael.Gregory/files/
Bio%20100/Bio%20100%20Lectures/Organ%20Systems/
Circulatory%20System/Circulatory%20System.htm

"The Circulatory System: The Circle of Blood." The Franklin Institute. Resources for Science Learning. 1996-2007.

http://www.fi.edu/learn/heart/systems/circulation.html

"Coronary Heart Disease." emedicineHealth.com. January 2006.

http://www.emedicinehealth.com/coronary_heart_disease/article_em.htm

"Diagnostic Tests and Procedures." Texas Heart Institute at St. Luke's Episcopal Hospital. July 2007.

http://texasheart.org/HIC/Topics/Diag/index.cfm

Harvard Medical School Family Health Guide. New York: Simon & Schuster, 2005.

"Heart Attack (Myocardial Infarction)." Medical Eds: Dennis Lee, MD and Daniel Kulick, MD. MedicineNet, Inc. April 2007.

http://www.medicinenet.com/heart_attack/page5.htm#tocg

"Heart Disease." Department of Health and Human Services. Centers for Disease Control and Prevention, Division for Heart Disease and Stroke Prevention. February 2007.

http://www.cdc.gov/DHDSP/library/fs_heart_disease.htm

"Heart Disease: Your Guide to Heart Disease." Web MD. Medical Ed.: Cynthia Haines, MD. June 2006.

http://www.webmd.com/content/pages/9/1675_57782.htm

"Heart and Vascular Diseases." Department of Health and Human Services National Institutes of Health, National Heart Lung and Blood Institute.

http://www.nhlbi.nih.gov/

"Introduction to Hematology." Puget Sound Blood Center, 1994-2006.

http://www.psbc.org/hematology/02_wbc.htm

"Introduction to the Circulatory System." "Your Guide to High Blood Pressure. Ed.: Craig Weber, MD. About.com Health. Disease and Conditions. November, 2006.

http://highbloodpressure.about.com/od/highbloodpressure101/p/circ_pro.htm

"Medicines by Design: The Biological Revolution in Pharmacology." National Institute of General Medical Sciences. National Institutes of Health. 2007.

http://www.healthieryou.com/rxdrugs.html

Neill, Catherine A. *The Heart of a Child: What Families Need to Know About Heart Disorders in Children*. Baltimore, MD: Johns Hopkins University Press, 2001.

"Yale University School of Medicine Heart Book." Medical Eds: Barry L. Zaret, M.D., Marvin Moser, M.D., Lawrence S. Cohen, M.D. New Haven: Yale University. 1992, rev. 2002.

http://www.med.yale.edu/library/heartbk/1.pdf

Index

About the Author

Ruth Bjorklund has written several books on science and health and lives on Bainbridge Island in Washington state with her husband, two children, and five pets. Living among tall trees and steep hills, she and her family try to stay heart healthy by walking, hiking, and being active outdoors.